SpringerBriefs in Education

For further volumes:
http://www.springer.com/series/8914

Frank Fischer · Fridolin Wild
Rosamund Sutherland · Lena Zirn

Grand Challenges in Technology Enhanced Learning

Outcomes of the 3rd Alpine Rendez-Vous

Springer

Frank Fischer
Ludwig-Maximilans-Universität München
Munich
Germany

Fridolin Wild
Knowledge Media Institute
The Open University
Milton Keynes
UK

Rosamund Sutherland
School of Education
University of Bristol
Bristol
UK

Lena Zirn
Department of Psychology
Ludwig-Maximilans-Universität München
Munich
Germany

ISSN 2211-1921 ISSN 2211-193X (electronic)
ISBN 978-3-319-01666-5 ISBN 978-3-319-01667-2 (eBook)
DOI 10.1007/978-3-319-01667-2
Springer Cham Heidelberg New York Dordrecht London

Library of Congress Control Number: 2013947052

Printed on acid-free paper

Springer is part of Springer Science+Business Media (www.springer.com)

Preface

Research challenges have helped to drive innovation beyond limits for a long time. The first recorded success story of such research competition is probably to be found in the prize-winning invention of the chronometer in 1773: the novel technology expanded horizons by rendering navigation at sea independent of a line of sight. More recently, i.e., half a century ago in 1961, boundaries were further lifted and research skyrocketed after the American president Kennedy set the Grand Challenge to put a man on the moon by the end of the decade. Only eight years later in 1969, Armstrong wrote history by making "one small step for [a] man, but one giant leap for mankind".

In the globalised world of today, however, the big problems we face and for which we need research are not up in the clouds or beyond the horizon—quite to the contrary!

Europe 2020, the EU's new strategy for a "smart, sustainable and inclusive economy",[1] for example, sets ambitious goals for Europe in education, innovation, employment, for the environment, and with respect to social inclusion.

Undoubtedly in a knowledge-driven society, technology-enhanced learning can play a major role in establishing a path towards achieving the targets in many of these areas.

For this reason, the Network of Excellence STELLAR has been established and contracted by the European Commission to (re-) structure the research field of technology-enhanced learning (TEL) by developing a new vision and building up the required capacities for approaching it.

This book presents a key piece of the vision and strategy developed in STELLAR. It sets out a new mid-term agenda by defining Grand Challenges for research and development in technology-enhanced learning. Other than mere technology prizes, STELLAR Grand Challenges deal with problems at the interface of social and technical sciences. They pose problems that can be solved only in interdisciplinary collaboration. The descriptions of the Grand Challenge Problems were sent out to a number of stakeholders from industry, academia, and policy-making, who responded with insightful, creative and critical comments bringing in their specific perspectives.

---

[1] http://ec.europa.eu/europe2020.

This book should inspire everyone interested in TEL and its neighbouring disciplines in their future projects. For all of the listed problems, first hints in respect to the approach, measurable success indicators and funding sources are sketched. The challenges focus on what these experts regard as important upcoming, pending, and innovative fields of research, the solution of which is within reach in a timeframe of 2–15 years starting right now!

This book should be a valuable resource not only to researchers and funding agencies, but also to teachers, and providers in formal education and continuing professional development.

History has shown us that Grand Challenges can be used successfully as an agenda-setting instrument. Focused campaigns in research and development can spark and coordinate global innovation by providing a reward mechanism complementing funding efforts.

Frank Fischer
Fridolin Wild
Lena Zirn
Rosamund Sutherland

Contents

Chapter 1
Grand Challenge Problems from the Alpine Rendez-Vous: An Introduction

1.1 The Concept of Grand Challenge Problems

Grand Challenge Problems have been used to catalyze advances in computer science, engineering, environmental science, and world health. Drawing on the work of Pea (2007), the STELLAR network has developed the idea of Technology Enhanced Learning (TEL) Grand Challenge Problems. These are fundamental socio-technical problems whose solution will lead to breakthroughs that improve learning and educational systems and bring long-term benefits to society (cf. U.S. Department of Education 2010).

TEL Grand Challenge Problems are understandable and timely and their solution is within-reach. The challenges have to be measurable and ideally can be achieved in incremental steps that produce useful outputs along the way.

TEL Grand Challenge Problems will need interdisciplinary coordinated efforts to be achieved, with groups of researchers and stakeholders working together towards the common goal of solving the problem. A crucial point is that 'the key paradox of interdisciplinary innovation is that one must plan for something one is not expecting' (Blackwell et al. 2009). Such work needs to recognise the range of issues that make interdisciplinary research difficult (Conole et al. 2010). In particular a recognition of the 'complex epistemological and methodological questions about the emergence, status, and validity of knowledge which constitute the background to a given discipline' (ibid, p 12).

Within STELLAR the formulation of TEL Grand Challenge Problems is linked to developing a mid-term agenda for TEL research in Europe and increasing the visibility of European TEL research. However the STELLAR Grand Challenge Problems are international in scope and of relevance globally.

The challenges presented in this book are not unrelated to each other. Their shared focus on technology-enhanced learning naturally ensures connections between them and the objectives they serve. STELLAR has established three guiding themes to reflect these connections and group together, that which belongs together.

F. Fischer et al., *Grand Challenges in Technology Enhanced Learning*,
SpringerBriefs in Education, DOI: 10.1007/978-3-319-01667-2_1,

These three themes deal with complementary aspects of technology-enhanced learning: connecting learners (2.1), orchestrating learning (2.2), and contextualising learning (2.3).

1.2 Development of the Grand Challenge Problems at the Alpine Rendez-Vous

The Grand Challenge Problems presented in this book originated from the Alpine Rendez-Vous 2011. An Alpine Rendez-Vous is a non-standard conference with two series of parallel but co-located workshops of 2 days that are coordinated with respect to their schedules. Each workshop was expected to develop at least one Grand Challenge Problem (GCP).

A common structure of the GCP and guidelines how to derive or design GCPs were provided (for the concept of the GCP see 1.1).

To facilitate the process, so-called provocateurs took part in the workshops. One provocateur was assigned per workshop in order to filter, collect, and provoke Grand Challenge discussion. The provocateurs were familiar with the concept of the Grand Challenge Problems. They informed about their role and tasks in an online meeting 2 weeks before the conference and in an additional briefing meeting online.

During the workshops, the provocateurs, tasks were to inform the workshop participants about the idea of GCPs as a workshop outcome, to facilitate contributions to discussions that relate to GCPs, and necessary, to formulate a Grand Challenge Problems draft and integrate feedback from the workshop participants.

Overall, a set of more than 30 Grand Challenge Problems was created during the Alpine Rendez-Vous. Afterwards, the GCPs were revised and similar GCPs were integrated resulting in the set of 22 Grand Challenge Problems in this book.

Chapter 2
Grand Challenge Problems from the Alpine Rendez-Vous

2.1 Grand Challenge Problems Focusing on Connecting Learners

STELLAR views learning as intimately connected with social interaction between people and as the continual construction of knowledge. New digital tools connect learners with other learners and teachers, trainers, experts or more knowledgeable others, helping them to communicate in effective ways, both to share and build knowledge. A wide variety of information and communication technologies (ICTs) connect people including web-based applications such as open and closed forums, personal or shared blogs, chat rooms, instant messaging and video conferences, tagging and collaborative text editing systems.

2.1.1 GCP1: Open Collaboration in Formal Education

Marie Joubert, Donatella Persico and Francesca Pozzi

It is generally recognized that, although online collaboration between learners has the potential to contribute to learning, teachers and learners do not fully appropriate the potential of this sort of activity (Reeves et al. 2004). Many innovations within this area have been developed and used in a variety of situations, but the online collaboration is not often sustained and learners frequently engage in the collaborative activity only to the extent that is required by the task or activity they are set. Take up is lower than hoped for. At the same time, there is evidence that many learners use social networking tools in their everyday lives, and there is a question within this research area related to ways in which formal education can draw on the power of social networking in order to optimise online collaborative activity for learning.

F. Fischer et al., *Grand Challenges in Technology Enhanced Learning*,
SpringerBriefs in Education, DOI: 10.1007/978-3-319-01667-2_2,

2.1.1.1 Problems of the European Education System Addressed, and Long Term Benefits for Society

The European education system values collaboration between learners. However, face-to-face collaboration limits learners to collaborating when they are co-located and collaborating only with other people within the location. Online collaboration has the potential to connect learners any time and any place, and to connect them with people they do not already know. However, it seems that teachers frequently need support in organising and structuring online collaborative activities for learning.

2.1.1.2 Main Activities to Address this Grand Challenge Problem

The program of research addressing this Grand Challenge Problem should include, but is not limited to, a comprehensive set of projects including innovations related to developing the approaches described above (which could include structuring or scripting the collaborative activities), quantitative and qualitative evaluations of these innovations, ethnographic studies to investigate the use of online collaborative tools in the everyday life of learners; evaluations and ethnographic studies should contribute to the iterative development of the innovations.

Those studies concerned with the structuring of online collaboration should address a tension between over-structuring (Dillenbourg 2002), which tends to leave students unmotivated, and under-structuring, which tends to leave students overwhelmed. It may be helpful to focus some studies on how structured activities are used by exploring how the structuring devices used are assimilated into student activity systems and are transformed from 'add-ons' to a way of doing things. Some studies might draw on the emerging '4T' model (Persico & Pozzi 2011), which structures online collaborative learning activity within four strands.

- The requirements of the learning 'task', including the activity type (e.g. jigsaw), the intended learning, formative and summative assessment, social and cognitive scaffolding, drawing on a repository of previously 'proven' building blocks.
- The 'timings' involved in the activity at all phases (before, during and after the activity), including adaptive teacher and computer interventions (feedback/support).
- The organisation of 'teams', which includes the teacher (if applicable) and the learners in dyads, small groups or larger groups flexibly adapting to unfolding situations.
- The 'technology' used, including hardware and software as well as other mediating artefacts such as visualisations/diagrams, particularly recognising the importance of learner agency in choosing (or not choosing) to use a particular technology.

2.1.1.3 Timeframe for the Grand Challenge Problem

The work for this Grand Challenge Problem would take up to 5 years, comprising two main phases. The first phase would study current practice, draw on lessons learnt and identification of 'what works' to devise and implement approaches to supporting teachers and learners, and evaluate interventions. The second phase would draw on the evaluations of the first phase to modify the designed approaches, re-implement and re-evaluate.

2.1.1.4 Measurable Progress and Success Indicators

Progress and success indicators will be related to individual initiatives within the programme. These will include (a) evaluation of the actual support provided to teachers and learners, from their perspectives, (b) the nature and extent of the online collaboration and (c) the level to which this collaboration is sustained. For example, within studies concerned with scripting/structuring online collaboration, measures of motivation and confusion could be used for "steering" short-term adjustments, and measures of reliance, appropriation, carry-on, and internalisation could be used for the major evaluation of success.

2.1.1.5 Attraction of Funding

European Funding sources would include the European Research Council or organizations such as Marie Curie. A concerted effort would also be made to encourage funding from respective National Research Councils. Exemplary bodies in the UK would be the Economic Research Council. There would also be funding possibilities from different stakeholders such as the Department for Education.

2.1.1.6 Connected Research Questions

- How do teachers manage the tension between structured activities and the need for fostering student agency in TEL?
- How could collaborative learning activities be designed and orchestrated to promote the learners' and learning communities' sense of ownership?
- To what extent should learners and learning communities be in control of the amount of structure they are provided with?
- What is the role of structuring techniques in different types of collaborative activities (e.g., exploring/relying/appropriating/internalizing/carrying-on activities)?
- What is the role of emotional/personal aspects in online collaboration?
- What is the role of cultural differences in online collaboration?
- What is the role of technology in online collaboration?

2.1.2 GCP2: Technology-Supported Representation-Fitness

Nicolas Balacheff

One of the challenges of teaching is finding a way to meaningfully introduce new representations to learners who do not already have particular representations (of a subject matter in their minds) or any prerequisites. This challenge is in one way or another common to all disciplines, but it is of special importance in science where representations are mostly strictly codified in semiotic registers and used for computational purposes. A badly introduced representation can be the source of misconceptions and exclusion of learners from the learning community, since adopting a representation is not only a cognitive but also a social process.

Hence, the challenge of the introduction must be rooted in a two-dimensional space: epistemological—understanding the role of the representation in the building and the use of a piece of knowledge—and sociological—understanding the communicative dimension of the representation and its contribution to the construction of a community. Problem-solving situations that involve communication are likely to provide the best context for facilitating the emergence, the sharing and the use of representations. This designates CSCL as the TEL research area in which tools and models could be found to take up this challenge.

This grand challenge problem is tightly related to the connecting learner and contextualizing learning Stellar Grand Challenges. It can be related to long-term basic research on meaning, learning and representation, and short-term research projects directly related to current technology seeking for its possible enhancement targeting first domain specific research projects where educational problems are well identified.

2.1.2.1 Addressed Problems of the European Education System and Long-Term Benefits to Society

This GCP problem is not specific to European education systems—it is of international relevance. It raises many issues, including the following, which are of interest for formal and informal education:

- For a given piece of knowledge, what would be the communication and problem-solving characteristics of a situation that support the emergence of a relevant and efficient shared representation?
- In the case of formal education, what constraints exist for an emergent representation that is either compliant to the socially shared one or that stands at a distance which allows the teacher to bridge the gap without "forcing" learners?
- In the case of informal learning, which hints would help to construct representations through processes allowing the management of tensions between a variety of individual needs and backgrounds and the construction of the community sharing meaning and knowledge?

2.1.2.2 Main Activities to Address this Grand Challenge Problem

From a scientific perspective, this challenge calls for a high-level input from semiology and epistemology in close relation to educational research and engineering. It requires computer scientists to better understand the interaction between knowledge representation, interface and its actual implementation. HCI requires epistemological characteristics, either reified or emergent of the interface and its system of interactions to be revisited and to produce models that take into account the "meaning" dimension and not only the functional dimension in computational terms ("meaning beyond affordance" may be the slogan).

The main activity should be a project (STREPS type) with a consortium attaining the previously-stated competence and a network of classroom or in-the-field learning communities to implement and evaluate the specifics of the situations. The content domain must be well defined and simple (esp. a domain in which the issue of representation is not completely open from the learning science and semiotic perspective).

2.1.2.3 Timeframe for the Grand Challenge Problem

This GCP can be associated with long-term basic research on meaning, learning and representation, and a short-term research project directly related to current technologies searching for its enhancement possibly targeting first domain specific research projects where educational problems are well identified.

A 3-years STREP would set a standard timeframe for a first demonstration.

2.1.2.4 Measurable Progress and Success Indicators

The explicit and precise description of the scenario for a successful learning situation that fulfils the mentioned properties and a consensus of the research community would be first evidence of success. A further indicator would be the level of dissemination and the activity of a community of teachers adopting these scenarios and engaging in discussions to understand and revise or improve them. Eventually, the adoption of the specification of scenarios to enhance CSCL environment making use of content-specific representations will be a relevant criterion.

2.1.2.5 Attraction of Funding

A progress on this issue will have an impact beyond education, on the design of advanced HCI principle of design for environments which will provide services but also evolve with the user understanding its function and functionalities. This may be of interest for the knowledge industry and fit well into the EC agenda.

2.1.2.6 Connected Research Questions

- What are communication and problem-solving characteristics of a situation that supports the understanding and sharing of a relevant representation?
- In the case of formal education, what are the constraints so that the emergent representation is either compliant to the one socially shared, or stands at a distance which allows the teacher to bridge the gap without "forcing" learners?
- In the case of informal learning, which hints would help to construct representations through processes allowing to manage the tensions between the variety of the individual prerequisites and the (re-) construction of the community's shared meaning and knowledge?

2.1.3 GCP3: Rich-Media Assignments

Daniel Spikol and Joshua Underwood

The widespread penetration of high-speed broadband Internet, WIFI infrastructure, fast mobile data networks combined with the fact that most people in OECD countries have data compatible mobile devices smart phones, tablets, and personal computers provides new opportunities for personally motivated education. In the emerging economies, many people have access to mobile phones and GSM coverage offers new avenues for learning. Yet, with all these technologies available to people of all ages there can be seen to be a clear lack of tools to inspire people to learn. Although digital based computer games, social networks for sharing rich media, and collaborative knowledge and news have vast audience participation, they can be seen to provide only a bare foundation for allowing people to construct personally meaningful rich-media. The grand challenge is to create socio-technical tools that inspire and motivate people to collaboratively and individually construct, create, and combine information like texts, websites, videos, audio, images together in new meaningful creations.

2.1.3.1 Problems of the European Education System Addressed, and Long Term Benefits for Society

Digital competences that enable individual and collaborative creativity and innovation are essential skills for future European citizens. School curriculums throughout the EU are being adopted to address the issue of these new digital skills. Despite these developments, recent studies have shown that most of the innovations related to the use of ICT in schools have not impacted pedagogical or school development as a whole. The problem is far from being trivial since online communication and interaction are no longer a separate phenomenon from children's daily lives. In this socio-technological configuration, schools in particular are deeply challenged as they are confronted with questions such as; What kinds of strategies and skills are learners developing outside schools? What are they learning in their interaction with digital tools? How are school practices and learning opportunities aligned to current and future individual, societal, and economical needs?

2.1.3.2 Main Activities to Address this Grand Challenge Problem

Currently, commercially available software for mobile devices are available to provide different types of data capture (video, images, text, location) and there is widespread use of social networks, but these different applications and services generally do not focus directly on educational outcomes. The challenge of harnessing creativity for education with mobile devices can be addressed from a design perspective by working across stakeholders to develop personally meaningful environments. The aim is to empower learners to become active in the process of pursuing personally meaningful problems, while providing enough support for their activity to result in the construction of useful knowledge and artefacts.

2.1.3.3 Timeframe for the Grand Challenge Problem

The work on this problem would take 2 years. The first year spent on investigating and evaluating international research projects, open-sourced and commercial products resulting in a state of the art and literature reviews along with guidelines for educational adoption. The second year would pragmatically attempt to develop a technical framework from these tools to be used in education. Throughout the project and in conjunction with different conferences and events, a series of structured 'hackathon' and design-based activities that bring together researchers, entrepreneurs, teachers, and young people will be held to align the exploratory and pragmatic activities.

2.1.3.4 Measurable Progress and Success Indicators

For the first year, the main output would be academic with peer review dissemination (publications and conferences) summarizing the availability, use, and impact of new mobile and ubiquitous tools for learner creation of artefacts. The second year will be a series of dissemination workshops, school implementations, and best practice guidelines that allow researchers and practitioners to work with the tools. The success of the challenge can be measured by research educational market adoption of the materials and practices.

2.1.3.5 Attraction of Funding

European funding sources would include the European Research Council and other funding European NGO agencies. Additional funding sources would include the Swedish Research Council, The Knowledge Foundation of Sweden, VINNOVA (Swedish Innovation Agency) plus national funding foundations along with Nordic Research Council.

2.1.3.6 Connected Research Questions

- What are the factors in technology-enhanced learning environments facilitating motivation and interest in learners of different ages?

2.1.4 GCP4: Supporting an Open Culture of Design for TEL

Yishay Mor

The last decade has seen a growing trend towards a shift in the perceived role of educators: from providers of knowledge to designers of learning activities. The call for such a repositioning of educators is heard from leaders in the field of TEL and resonates well with the growing culture of design-based research in education. Yet, it is still struggling to find a foothold in educational practice. We claim that the root cause for this discrepancy is the lack of appropriate representations of design knowledge in education, as well as the lack of tools to manipulate such representations.

Thus, we pose the following grand challenge: how do we create a platform for open, live, malleable, dynamic representation of design knowledge in TEL, supportive collaborative processes of design for learning, learning to design, and learning by design in such a way that includes the broadest community possible?

2.1.4.1 Problems of the European Education System Addressed and Long-Term Benefits for Society

The evolution and wide access of advanced technologies offer educators and learners unprecedented opportunities to create, organise, share and access knowledge. Such technologies effect potent learning environments, yet these are constantly shifting with increasing complexity. The challenge of education no longer revolves around the delivery of knowledge: it is about designing environments, tools and activities for learners to construct knowledge.

An open platform for learning design might promote the emergence of a new culture of educational practice, in which expertise is rapidly and effectively shared, critiqued and aggregated. It will lead to the wide proliferation of cost-effective and robust educational practices that make effective use of technological advances as they appear.

A design attitude should not be pre-conditioned by technical ability: it may well be reflected in effective configuration and customisation of existing resources. Over the last few decades, the design paradigm in TEL research has achieved a growing momentum. However, in order for it to attain its full desired impact, it needs to develop a common language and make this language accessible to the widest possible audience. Such a language, as well as the related media of interaction, should allow experts and novices to extract design knowledge from experience, articulate it in a coherent manner, connect, combine and manipulate it, and use it to resolve new challenges.

2.1.4.2 Main Activities to Address this Grand Challenge Problem

In order for educators to effectively orchestrate learning within this landscape, they need to perceive themselves, and indeed to be perceived by society, as techno-pedagogical designers. A design attitude should be reflected in the production of new resources, as well as in effective configuration and customisation of existing ones. The design paradigm has established itself in TEL research. Yet, for it to attain its full desired impact, it needs to develop a common language and make this language accessible to the widest possible audience. Such a language, and the related media of interaction, should allow experts and novices to extract design knowledge from experience, articulate it in a coherent manner, connect, combine and manipulate it, and use it to resolve new challenges.

This language should be supported by appropriate tools and community spaces, which will streamline the process of constructing, validating and utilising design knowledge, making it open, accessible and transparent. It cannot be a uniform, centralised entity—but needs to allow for a diverse discourse by establishing a set of open protocols and standards over which an open process of massively collaborative knowledge building can thrive. This process needs to be embedded in the culture of the professional community.

2.1.4.3 Timeframe for the Grand Challenge Problem

The development of an open platform for learning design requires the co-evolution of representations, tools and practices. It needs to proceed iteratively and synchronously on all fronts. To reach maturity, it would require four annual iterations, scaling up from an initial pilot to a pan-European community of learning designers.

2.1.4.4 Measurable Progress and Success Indicators

The success of such an initiative will be measured by the vibrancy of the community it engenders, the evolution of a widespread culture of learning design, and consequently, the quantity and quality of open learning design artefacts. Exemplary success indicators include:

- **Vibrancy**: an established community of several hundred educators across Europe actively engaged in collaborative design.
- **Culture**: evidence of learning design vocabulary and practices emerging in professional texts and beyond the core community.
- **Artefacts**: a growing open repository of design objects and educational resources, judged by peers and experts to be of high quality.

2.1.4.5 Attraction of Funding

In order to succeed, such an endeavour requires a truly interdisciplinary effort combining social science (understanding the community aspects), computer science (developing the tools) and design research (developing the representations and co-ordinating the efforts). An open, participatory culture of learning design can yield commercial outputs and therefore potentially attract private funding from publishers. It would benefit NGOs committed to educational agendas and could draw on their contributions. Nevertheless, it is expected that the main investment will come from national and European public funding. A possible solution for sustaining the platform is the creation of an open market for learning design.

2.1.4.6 Connected Research Questions

- What are the appropriate forms for representing design knowledge in TEL, and how could these be effectively blended into the discourse and practices of educators, researchers and policy makers?
- How can we empower and support educational practitioners in reshaping their role from providers of knowledge to designers of technology-enhanced learning experiences?
- How can we evaluate the quality of design products and processes in TEL and assess their impact on learning?

2.1.5 GCP5: Multi-Level Evaluations of TEL

Anders D. Olofsson, J. Ola Lindberg and Trond E. Hauge

To improve the conditions for TEL, there is a need to constantly address the rapid increase in the up-take and use of digital technologies in European schools and to understand how learning take place at different levels. But understanding conditions is not enough; the use of technologies need to be understood in order to provide understandings of the learning they can enhance across institutional levels. The underpinning idea is that technologies do more than just support learning; they change how we think and act as humans and the ways we interpret and develop learning.

2.1.5.1 Problems of the European Education System Addressed and Long-Term Benefits for Society

Research in relation to up-take and use of digital technologies for improving TEL and knowledge building in European schools seems to be neither clear nor indicative of a full-scale success. Reasons for this could include the tendencies in research of focusing on possible indicators to locate in every single school and a lack of intersectional research, i.e. by overlooking the interplay between organizational structure and culture. To this day, few studies provide insight and understanding of critical factors for TEL at the institutional level. New methodological approaches are needed for evaluating and researching TEL in European schools.

2.1.5.2 Main Activities to Address this Grand Challenge Problem

These approaches need to include a multi-level focus that takes into account the motivators for various stakeholders in the European school system. The use of multi-level methodologies will facilitate the producing of evaluations and research results that allow each set of school stakeholders to feel that their stake is being addressed. Since motivation differs between stakeholders, it is necessary to develop research on TEL in participatory designs assuring joint interests and agreement of stakeholders. Otherwise, we end up with an effective methodology for evaluating an initiative that the stakeholders do not buy into. The development of a multi-level methodological approach will produce new insight regarding TEL and the use of digital technologies in schooling and education, on how technologies are constructed and how knowledge develops across levels. Constructing evaluations using multi-level approaches allows for complex interactions between policy makers, strategic school leadership, teachers and students to be negotiated successfully. These evaluations have the potential to lead to a better understanding of the use of technology and how it can enhance learning in and between institutional levels in European schools.

2.1.5.3 Timeframe for the Grand Challenge Problem

Evaluations covering institutional complexities and practices in school will take time to produce. They need to rest on rich data sets within each level and in relation to the other levels. The estimated time needed to produce results of great impact and relevance for European schools is 42 months.

2.1.5.4 Measurable Progress and Success Indicators

To measure progress and success will require a longitudinal approach. Indicators that can be used include:

- Increased acceptance among stakeholders of looking at intersectional practices in the planning and evaluation of TEL in schools.
- The development of a research body comprising a rich set of data providing insight and understanding of critical factors for the use of digital technologies across institutional levels.
- New and innovative methods to develop knowledge on TEL and digital technologies are increasingly reported in scientific journals.
- The relevance of research results is validated by teachers and pupils through surveys and case studies.

2.1.5.5 Attraction of Funding

Providing research capacities in the form of new innovative methods for researching TEL will have to rely on partnerships that include participants that display variation and similarities, as well as answers to a design that include different forms of uniqueness. This can be fruitfully developed through partnerships that can be found in already existing networks. The EC would be responsible for developing the future research capacities for Europe in this regard, preferably within the research frameworks and dissemination through the programs for education, training, and lifelong learning.

2.1.5.6 Connected Research Question

- How can we design multi-level methodologies that provide possibilities to study intersectional TEL practices at an institutional level sensible to the complexities of interactions between policy, strategic leadership, teacher and student?

2.1.5.7 Guest Commentaries on Connecting Learners

Roy Pea is David Jacks Professor of Education and the Learning Sciences at Stanford University, and has published widely on K-12 learning and education,

especially in science, math and technology, fostered by advanced technologies including scientific visualization, virtual communities, digital video collaboratories and mobile ICT. He is a Fellow of the National Academy of Education, Association for Psychological Science, the American Educational Research Association, and is co-author of the 2010 National Education Technology Plan for the US Department of Education. In 2004–2005, Roy was President of the International Society for the Learning Sciences.

Dr Michelle Selinger is the Director of Education Practice for the Global Public Sector practice of the Cisco Internet Business Solutions Group (IBSG). She focuses on technology-enabled education transformation in formal education.

Elisavet Linou was a policy advisor on innovation to Greek Prime Minister Georgios Papandreou, from 2009 to 2011. Her projects included work on public sector reform, social innovation, and technology in education. She now conducts research on public sector innovation at Harvard University, Cambridge, MA.

2.1.6 Guest Commentary by Roy Pea

STELLAR's teams developed five important GCPs on "connected learners": knowledge representation (GCP1), empowering collaborative learning (GCP2), fostering learner motivation with mobile tools (GCP3), supporting design knowledge building (GCP4), and multi-level TEL evaluations (GCP5). My aim is to provide supportive admiration and constructive critiques to advance these well-merited enterprises.

I enthusiastically foreground the GCPs' core assumption that learning is grounded in social interaction and knowledge building, shared by our LIFE Center—an NSF-funded multi-disciplinary center developing and testing principles on the social foundations of human learning in informal and formal environments, with the goal of enhancing human learning from infancy to adulthood. While we do not examine only technology-enhanced learning, my reflections derive from the cumulative experience of our 8 years in tackling related issues.

GCP1 asks how to "meaningfully introduce new [knowledge] representations when… learners do not have this representation"—and acknowledges the cognitive and social dimensions of learners' appropriation of the new semiotic resources provided in cultural practices with symbol systems. Such challenges arise whether representations are expressed on computer or paper (e.g. algebraric equations, Cartesian coordinate graphs, Newtonian force diagrams). It may be useful reframing this GCP in terms of what design principles and tools should guide our pedagogical practices for learners to develop competencies in problem solving with novel knowledge representational media. Progress on this question must wrangle with the research literature on "learning progressions", domain by domain.

GCP2 is about empowering learners to collaborate. Yet part of what learners need to learn is when collaboration is warranted. The authors bemoan that "take up is lower than hoped for" in online collaboration, but the basic question we must ask, which may reframe GCP2, is: how, given the competencies of a group of learners who seek to solve a given problem in a domain together, should the tools of the problem-solving environment be configured to optimally support their productive collaborative processes? Scripting support or not as the needs require would be embodied in answering that question. Collaboration in and of itself is not the goal, but can serve as a well-adapted means to specific ends that the collaborative constellation can realize in its processes and outcomes.

GCP3 has a forked definition; asking both how can ICT tools motivate people to learn and inquire, and how to create tools allowing people to create their own multimedia information resources. While each is important, it was less clear how reviewing the plethora of existing digital media production environments (in the hundreds to thousands) would lead to guidelines for educational adoption of the latter, or inform the first question.

If I understand GCP4, it asks how to establish broadly useful open tools for representing design knowledge to advance education. GCP4 is preoccupied calling for a single common language to "extract design knowledge from experience" and encompass all techno-pedagogical needs of educators, whatever their educational domains. We need justification for why a single language is required or why it is considered feasible, given the diversity of knowledge domains for which TEL environments need to be established.

GCP5 proposes multi-level TEL evaluations resonating with needs of students, teachers, education leadership and education policymakers. Defining relationships between existing summative assessment systems and prospective TEL formative assessments that can help educators guide learning progress for all students will be central to this quest, calling on the emerging field of learning analytics to provide interactive data visualizations to serve all stakeholders in educational systems.

2.1.7 Guest Commentary by Michelle Selinger

Technology coupled with research on the brain has made us more critical of the resources available for learning and more cognisant of what might be needed in order to make leaning more robust, more meaningful and more effective. The Grand Challenge Problems under the heading of connecting learners each address this issue.

Balacheff describes the problem of representation. His problem is made more complex by the mix of cultures that learners now engage with. The world is a global classroom and the learners' social, economic and cultural environment will dictate the nature of how a representation is created (Selinger 2004). Trying to make this representation work across cultures that differ widely becomes even more complex and less easy to share than when the classroom was a local affair. The complexity of this problem becomes even larger but has to be addressed in a networked society.

The challenge of rich-media assignments is an interesting one, not because of the paucity of tools, but because of the problems of assessment. There are rich media tools emerging and others available that address the challenge of rich media, and it is possible that some adaptations are possible in others with little effort and cost to make these tools more usable and acceptable by educators. However, this Grand Challenge Problem needs to be associated with research on leaning analytics in addition to the challenge it is trying to address, because however good the tools are, their use will be trivialised if robust assessment strategies are not developed at the same time. So far digital assessment tools are mainly used for formative assessment in schools, and rarely for summative assessment.

In supporting an open future for design, this challenge could benefit from looking at what we have learnt from open source development and from Logo,

Scratch and other such communities. There are a number of design tools and resources available on the web, but without the development of a toolbox that is easy to learn, easy to use and open to all formats. There are more digital resources on the web than any one teacher can ever use, but locating them, adapting them to a pedagogical model tailored to learner needs, and finding ways to use them effectively is the ultimate Grand Challenge.

Finding a solution to this problem (and the one of assessment) will ensure technology becomes firmly embedded in the curriculum, and transforms teachers from delivery machines to curators of the learning environment. If this can happen, and with a multidisciplinary team of researchers, educators, games designers, filmmakers, programmers and, of course, students, then we will see the sea change we have all been waiting for. It will take extensive resources but I believe it can be achieved.

The final challenge in this section concerns multi-level approaches to evaluations of TEL. This problem might be more easily addressed if TEL was disaggregated. TEL is multifaceted, yet we consider it as one entity. How can learning through online collaboration technologies, for example, be compared to the learning that takes place through playing a single player educational game? Are the methodologies for evaluating them the same?

In summary, these problems are undoubtedly problems that need to be addressed and each will have a bearing on the efficacy of the other if they were indeed solved.

2.1.8 Guest Commentary by Elisavet Linou (Policy Advisor on Innovation, Greek Government)

Amidst an ongoing European crisis, the significance of connected learning in Europe moves beyond the classroom. The very nature of connectedness inspires a series of policy questions: can we utilise open platforms to build equity as well as achievement? Can the formal educational system mirror digital collaboration outside schools? Ultimately, can Europe utilise connectedness to become more competitive?

The five GCPs presented above are exciting, from a policy perspective, because they represent a shift in how we view TEL, as well as a fresh perspective on where European educational systems can go. From these challenges, three policy imperatives emerge:

(A) Design platforms that allow for their own malleability.

By focusing on an open culture of TEL design, the benefit of creating digital platforms lies not only in the power of co-creation, but in the ability of such systems to evolve as does society (and education). The first question, then, is how we can integrate these "socio-technical" tools of flexibility into an institutionally heavy educational system. The follow up question is how to encourage the players in these networks to be equally flexible and malleable. That is, the grand challenges lend themselves to future research on the training of how can we help teachers to utilize these platforms effectively, and adapt their teaching practices as knowledge evolves.

(B) Design innovative policies that allow for their own evaluation.

It is refreshing to see that the formulation of GCPs include evaluation in the very design of the research question. Designing policy by first studying the evidence base is perhaps the most important trend in policy making. Proposing, a GCP that is wholly dedicated to multi-level evaluations of TEL, captures a key policy challenge. We just don't have enough information about how institutions can shape, hinder, or support the growth of effective TEL. By making evaluation a key component of the research agenda, rather than a mere supplement to innovations, this GC becomes directly relevant to the future of TEL promotion, at the institutional level.

But there are another component to the evaluation agenda. Beyond the clear academic benefits, the very nature of connected learning may benefit from inward evaluation. To the fascinating 4T model presented in GCP1, we could add a fifth "T": trial. That is, using TEL, we have the capacity to make trial and error—internal evaluation—part of the learning process. Supporting experimentation from the learners themselves is, after all, the key to innovation.

(C) Create new communities through digital interaction.

The last, and perhaps most central policy imperative reflects the potential of connected learning to build communities. As many GCPs suggest, digital interaction creates the space for new definitions of communities. Politically, this may spell a transformation in how learners of today define their communities and peers tomorrow. Socially, we may see new community lines cut across previous economic or ethnic boundaries. The only danger is that the creation of dynamic digital communities may translate into a new digital divide, either in the community of learners, or in the community of teachers. As such, there exists a complementary policy challenge to ensure that entry or exit into digital communities is costless to all.

Ultimately, there is a deeper behavioural question about why people participate in collaborative communities. How are amazing examples of collaborative learning, like Wikipedia, even possible? How can we create an educational system that at the very least mirrors, and at the very most enhances this process? The power of TEL to change how we interact and learn, combined with the power of research to shape how policy-makers design institutions, may spell out a new era of innovation for Europe. If anything can pull Europe's out of its current crisis, it is the ability of the next generation to build real capital out of a network of ideas.

2.2 Grand Challenge Problems Focusing on Orchestrating Learning

STELLAR uses the term 'orchestrating' to refer to the design of learning situations, taking into account the learners, the role of the teacher or trainer, the role of assessment and the digital and non-digital tools used. In orchestrating learning, attention is paid to all these aspects of the situation and, importantly, to the relationship between them. Traditional models of teaching often need re-thinking when digital tools are included in the range of tools within the learning situation. For example, ICT provides multiple possibilities for learners to access knowledge that traditionally would have been provided by the teacher.

2.2.1 GCP6: Emotion-Adaptive TEL

Gill Clough

The way we learn is influenced by the emotions we experience. Raised levels of stress and anxiety can lead to poorer performance. Low levels of arousal or engagement can affect our concentration and have a negative impact on how we take on new knowledge.

Technology enhanced learning (TEL) research is founded on the premise that technological developments offer new and often unanticipated ways to improve the ways we teach and learn. These developments often occur in fields other TEL, and their implications for teaching and learning can be profound. For example, in the medical field, bio-sensor technology designed to record physiological responses now incorporate substantial on-board data storage. They have been miniaturised to such and extent that they can be worn inconspicuously during everyday activities. The primary purpose of these devices is to aid in the diagnosis and monitoring of physiological responses, however some of these physiological responses are indicative of the emotional reactions, which may be influencing our learning.

Such sensors offer insights into the physiological impacts of learning with TEL. They can act as diagnostic instruments to enable us to identify the impact of emotional responses on learning. They can also act as learning aids which use bio-feedback to reinforce learning or identify problems areas.

2.2.1.1 Problems of the European Education System Addressed, and Long Term Benefits for Society

Learners respond to teaching and the curriculum not only with cognition but also emotion. Fear of maths is one example. Emotional responses could be positive, to successful and engaging teaching, negative, or a more complex mixture of pleasure, wonder, anxiety, stress and fear. The challenge is to understand how emotions form part of teaching and learning, and to harness the power of emotions to enable fulfilling and productive learning experiences.

2.2.1.2 Main Activities to Address this Grand Challenge Problem

From a theoretical perspective, managing emotions can be regarded as a second order cybernetic process. We react directly to stimuli, including complex experiences such as classroom lessons, with psycho-physical responses. As cognitive beings, we have the ability to reflect on these experiences, at the time or later. Technology could intervene in this process in a number of ways. If learners can be equipped with devices that measure their immediate emotional responses, these could be made visible to themselves and others. Direct measurements could be made of pulse-rate or galvanic skin conductance, e.g. with a wristband worn by each learner that glows in different colours indicating types of emotional arousal. Learners, in a maths lesson could reflect and respond to the emotions of themselves and others in productive ways.

The emotions made visible by technology might be used for self monitoring, as for example with the 'talk table' developed by Dillenbourg and colleagues where a meeting table responds to the amount of talk from each participant, shown by an arrays of glowing lights at each place round the table. As they gain a visual indication of how much they are talking, the participants can decide how to adjust their behaviour. Similarly, in a classroom, if devices can be constructed that indicate each learner's anxiety or stress, then that could form part of self-regulation by the learners, or management by the teacher. Another opportunity for technology enhancement is capture streams of emotion data from each participant in a teaching session and then employ data mining techniques to explore relations between teaching events and emotional responses. A more speculative application could be to explore what the poet Wordsworth described as "emotion recollected in tranquillity". To inspire his poetry, Wordsworth would commune with nature until it evoked a strong emotional response, then he would hurry home and try to recreate that emotion, to inspire the poetry. A similar effect might be possible through some technology-enabled mood inducement, where learners 'store up' emotional responses during a teaching session then re-create them later, as part of reflecting on their learning.

The ethical challenges of harnessing emotions for learning are as great as the technical and logistic ones. As human beings, we have the ability to hide and manipulate our emotions. What are the consequences of, literally, wearing our emotions on our sleeves? Even if such emotional enhancement of learning were technically feasible, would it be ethically acceptable? Could mood-monitoring, or mood-inducing, technology ever have a place in the classroom?

2.2.1.3 Timeframe for the Grand Challenge Problem

As technology developments move at a fast pace, we can expect rapid changes in the types of physiological responses we can collect, and in the ease with which we can collect them. However the ethical challenges that emerge as we attempt to harness these technologies for learning make it unwise to attempt to implement a "quick fix". As such, the expected timeframe for addressing this Grand Challenge problem is in the region of 3–5 years.

2.2.1.4 Measurable Progress and Success Indicators

- A series of research studies that provide evidence to support the hypothesis that there is a relationship between physiological data, emotional responses and learning.
- Learning interventions designed or adapted to incorporate bio-signals as described above.
- A coherent set of ethical guidelines for this work.

2.2.1.5 Attraction of Funding

ESRC, ERC, EU.

2.2.1.6 Connected Research Questions

- What is the relationship between physiological response as measured through, say, heart-rate variability or galvanic skin response, and learning?
- Does an awareness of physiological responses to learning activities have an impact on learning?
- Can we use the relationship between physiological response and learning to create more effective learning activities?

2.2.2 GCP7: Assessment and Automated Feedback

Denise M. Whitelock

The GCP formulated by participants of the assessment strand of the NGTEL workshop at ARV2011 is looking at a time perspective of about 10–15 years. The GCP is based on the aim of breaking current limitations in terms of the learning domains, the attention to summative assessment in current educational practices and last but not least the limitation to focus on traditional question-formats (e.g. multiple choice). The final aim of addressing this GCP is to change the perception of assessment from a judging instrument to a support mechanism for learning.

2.2.2.1 Problems of the European Education System Addressed, and Long Term Benefits for Society

The problem addressed is to leverage the motivating effect of assessment which we know drives learning (Rowntree 1987) away from such an onerous task for students into a real learning experience where self awareness and profitable direction of learning can take place through engaging in a process that supports a meta-cognitive appraisal of "Assessment for Learning".

2.2.2.2 Main Activities to Address this Grand Challenge Problem

The GCP can be addresses by wide-scale development, evaluation and implementation of new formative assessment scenarios including the development and evaluation of technologies that make for example intensive use of text-/data mining or natural language processing approaches. A European challenge is to develop tools and methods that can cover a wide range of European languages.

2.2.2.3 Timeframe for the Grand Challenge Problem

The timeframe is about 10–15 years to build these assessment/automatic feedback systems.

2.2.2.4 Measurable Progress and Success Indicators

Success can be measured if we can prove that learners recognize the value of formative assessment for their own learning. Some effects that can be measured include:

- Increased motivation during the assessment situation.
- Changed role of assessment from a process learners have to do to a process learners want to do.
- Decreased drop-out rates in distance learning programs.
- Second-order effects on summative assessment.

2.2.2.5 Attraction of Funding

The European Research Council and National Bodies such as the EPSRC in the UK need to be persuaded to fund this type of research since in the long term assisting students to understand how they learn will provide an adaptive and flexible European work force.

2.2.2.6 Connected Research Questions

- What are components and stages of assessment literacy and how can it be supported with novel language technologies?
- How can technology help to assess affective and psychomotor learning?

2.2.3 GCP8: One Informed Tutor per Child

Effie L.-C. Law, Felix Mödritscher, Martin Wolpers, Denis Gillet and Fridolin Wild

Human tutors can be assisted by technology to help learners become more competent and meet the demands of our knowledge-driven society. An individual tutor for every child in Europe (and beyond) is a desideratum that has not yet been realized. With the help of predictive models and learning analytics, this area could be significantly strengthened. Combining agents and human tutors to provide high quality tutoring to every child can be achieved.

2.2.3.1 Problems of the European Education System Addressed and Long-Term Benefits for Society

How well students will do at, e.g., lower secondary education, is still strongly shaped by their family characteristics. The expansion of university education over the last decades has brought most benefits for households with better educated parents (Machin 2006). For example, children with university-educated parents are much more likely to go to university than others (Machin 2006). This is often attributed to differences in cognitive and non-cognitive skills. Nonetheless, teachers, tutors, and other key persons in the social network of learners (including even peers) are often overwhelmed by large volumes of (unorganized) learning resources, on the one hand, and lack time and effort to assist individual or group tutoring, on the other. Improving support systems for tutoring can help make a difference by increasing the quality of tutoring and—ultimately—by enabling more people to become facilitators of learning.

2.2.3.2 Main Activities to Address this Grand Challenge Problem

This involves the research of:

Research and development of predictive models targeting predicting performance based on traces is needed. This involves a change from the status quo which largely focuses on descriptive models.

Entrance barriers for innovative new research need to be lowered by providing organised evaluation forums to competitively test predictive models, thereby making different solutions comparable via key benchmarks. Such evaluation competitions are available in other fields: e.g. search engines are evaluated in yearly cycles (with varying focus points) in TREC (Text Retrieval Conference) and CLEF (Cross-Language Evaluation Forum). Evaluations can be done along two lines: accuracy versus satisfaction. This involves developing shared methodologies for evaluating effectiveness gain for teachers and learners. Learning analytics need to be developed that provide intuitive graphical user interfaces that foster quick understanding of performance supported by aesthetic displays. Feedback needs to be provided to support analyses in real-time. Pedagogically sound user interfaces need to be developed.

Research and development would benefit from open requirements elicitation along implementation competitions in the bartering platforms for software development; this requires requirements modelling methods and support facilities such as helpdesk monitoring.

Since data gathering and analysis of personal learning experiences is involved in this kind of endeavours, research on digital identity, privacy, and trust is needed to investigate ethical implications and to elaborate models that are in accordance with existing laws.

A set of traces (with objective, human assessed performance scores) can be provided to evaluate the predictive models/learning analytics. A test set (with non-disclosed human performance scores) can be retained to be used in a competition.

2.2.3.3 Timeframe for the Grand Challenge Problem

This could be realised within a timeframe of 3–5 years. As a game changer in existing research, lasting impact would provide continued innovation on a broader horizon.

2.2.3.4 Measurable Progress and Success Indicators

The availability of standardised data sets that include objective data derived from specific certain evaluation measures such as task completion rate and raw traces of learning activities can be monitored. Evaluation methodologies can be developed and documented in publications. The effectiveness and efficiency of predictive models can be evaluated with this and a high level of, accuracy can be determined as a threshold for success. Target benchmarks can iteratively be increased in continuous evaluation forums. User interfaces and visual learning analytics are more difficult to evaluate and require qualitative methods with trials.

2.2.3.5 Attraction of Funding

EU ICT funding should be targeted as it provides the right mix of research & development combined with strong exploitation and dissemination. National funding such as DFG (Germany) and EPSRC (UK) provide alternatives focusing on national focuses and interest.

2.2.3.6 Connected Research Question

- How can advances in computer science and human–computer interaction (including developments such as text classification, predictive models, learning analytics, agents) be used to support human tutors to facilitate learning in their tutees?

2.2.4 GCP9: Improving Educational Practices Through Data-supported Information Systems

Hendrik Drachsler

2.2.4.1 Problems of the European Education System Addressed and Long-Term Benefits for Society

In order to make data supported information systems an effective tool for educational practice, various limitations and hurdles in technology, privacy and education need to be addressed. It is important to realise that data-supported tools work with computational results that are not easy to understand and need to be presented in an easy way (e.g., by visualizations) to address the daily practice of the educational stakeholders. It is crucial to interpret the presented outcomes in a correct manner to take the right follow-up activities that can lead to improved learning. Therefore, the interpretation of educational data and its related tools requires new competences to deal with the outcomes (statistical knowledge, critical thinking, privacy awareness and ethical competences).

2.2.4.2 Main Activities to Address this Grand Challenge Problem

- Developing new data-driven tools that are easy to understand.
- Make new real time data tools available as test applications.
- Identify suitable algorithms and map them to certain datasets and learning purposes.
- Integrate statistical, critical thinking, privacy awareness and ethical competences into the teacher education programs.

2.2.4.3 Timeframe for the Grand Challenge Problem

The development of the data tools has already started: at every conference, new data-driven tools are presented (Zhang and Almeroth 2010). Systems like Mendeley and open access journals already show us the future of academic work. The training of the new competencies for teachers and students in the primary and secondary education level will take more time (5–10 years) with having many different levels in the EU partner countries.

2.2.4.4 Measurable Progress and Success Indicators

- An increased effectiveness, efficiency or satisfaction of the learning process.
- Courses for educational providers that train competencies to handle data products.
- An increasing amount of data mash up systems for different educational stakeholders (students, teachers, parents and educational providers).

2.2.4.5 Attraction of Funding

The Lifelong Learning Programme of the EU is suitable for the competence training. The development of the new data driven tools can be funded by FP7 and national calls.

2.2.4.6 Connected Research Questions

- Based on the experiences with SCORM and IMS-LD that should have created a European Learning Object market, will a common dataset format really lead to more datasets in TEL?
- What are the barriers to a broader use of data sharing opportunities, and what are measures to overcome these barriers?
- How can we deal with the diversity of data from various TEL systems? What are appropriate levels of granularity?

2.2.5 GCP10: Semiotic Recommender Systems for Learning

Nicolas Balacheff

Technology offers a wide range of possibilities to represent learning objects and content, either in texts, hypertexts, drawings, animations and films. All these representations present advantages and limits that are rarely presented precisely to teachers who have to choose material for their daily teaching. This choice is very complex because of the many aspects to be taken into account: nature of the content to be taught, variety of the available resources (computers, digital tablets, smart phones, phones, pocket calculators, paper & pencil), constraints on the communication (on site, at a distance, with or without shared visualizations), learners' competencies and needs. An ideal scenario would include teachers describing the content and the constraints and then getting advice about the representations that would best fit their students' learning needs. Furthermore, they would express these needs and get the resources that best fit the requirements overall.

2.2.5.1 Problems of the European Education System Addressed and Long-Term Benefits for Society

This GCP is not specific to European education systems, but is of international relevance. The problem consists in a "data overflow" and the difficulty of finding the proper resources on the Internet. The long-term benefit is the enhancement of the teachers' professional activities and a more efficient exploitation of the Internet's learning potential. With learners able to express their needs, one may expect such a system to provide responses to a question by selecting the most adapted representation. This technology may not only impact learning, but also the use of the Internet within an informal learning context.

2.2.5.2 Main Activities to Address this Grand Challenge Problem

From a scientific perspective, this challenge calls for a high level of collaboration between computer scientists and researchers with specific expertise in semantic, learning science, semiotic and epistemology. The main activity should be a project (STREPS type) with a consortium gathering the above-stated competencies and, as a key outcome, a prototype of such a tool in a well-defined and simple domain (esp. a domain in which the issue of representation is not completely open from the learning science and semiotic perspective).

Additionally, related research projects could be designed to explore the following complementary features:

- Indicators to recognize the right moment/time to provide non-intrusive feedback/scaffolding to learners.
- Indicators on when, how, and what kind of structuring the learning process should be provided in a personalized way.
- Criteria for choosing the effective order of representation type (self-constructed created versus pre-constructed given) that depends on the expected processing and conceptual understanding of the learner.

2.2.5.3 Timeframe for the Grand Challenge Problem

A 3-years EU-funded project (STREP).

2.2.5.4 Measurable Progress and Success Indicators

Running a prototype in a non-trivial knowledge domain would be a good indication of success, together with an acceptable argumentation regarding its potential generalizability.

2.2.5.5 Attraction of Funding

This idea could attract funding from the knowledge industry and Ministries of Education of EU member states. Such a problem can be the origin of successful European projects (STREP size).

2.2.5.6 Connected Research Questions

- What are indicators to recognize the right moment/time to provide non-intrusive feedback/scaffolding to learners?
- What are criteria for choosing the order of different representation types (e.g., self-constructed created versus pre-constructed given) depending on the expected processing and conceptual understanding of the learner in TEL environments?

2.2.6 GCP11: Enhancing Learning with Improved Information Retrieval

Hendrik Drachsler

2.2.6.1 Problems of the European Education System Addressed and Long-Term Benefits for Society

Europe's education systems suffer from decreasing amount of teachers and the request to increase the amount of high-educated students in a short time period. As a consequence, there is less time for the individual support of students and the teaching quality continues to decrease. On the other hand, the education systems are increasingly based on electronic systems like LMS and e-portfolios. With the increase in available educational data, the application of information retrieval technologies becomes valuable to create new services for the educational stakeholders (students, parents, teachers, and educational institutes). The combination of educational data and information retrieval techniques, also known as Learning Analytics (LA), will become a powerful tool in educational practice and student guidance (Johnson et al. 2011). LA promises the educational field reduced delivery costs, more effective learning environments and experiences, accelerated development of competencies, and increased collaboration between students and teachers.

But LA also has barriers and limitations. Among these are issues of privacy and data protection that need to be addressed by policy guidelines. Additionally, challenges arise with respect to data surveillance[1] (social sorting, cumulative disadvantages) and its ethical implications.

2.2.6.2 Main Activities to Address this Grand Challenge Problem

- In order to discuss and improve the above-mentioned situation, a new vocabulary needs to be accomplished in order to discuss privacy, data protection and surveillance issues. Among others, the following question arises: what are better terms for expressing concepts like ownership and access control when the replication and distribution of digital systems is so easy that the concepts have no traction?
- Research on how existing privacy and transparency solutions can be integrated in dataTEL practice and how state of the art security solutions can be used to secure large educational datasets is needed.
- There is a need for data awareness education for society. Such an educational program should not be limited to teaching individuals when to reveal or conceal their data, but also to increase their understanding of large datasets, surveillance practices, and related problems.
- User and stakeholder studies (case studies) are necessary to understand complex requirements for privacy, data protection, and surveillance in dataTEL.
- Issues surrounding privacy, data protection, and surveillance need to be addressed from the beginning of the research and not as an add-ons. Methodologies and guidelines that support this vision need to be developed to support privacy and ethical practices.
- There needs to be research on how to bridge the gap between dataTEL researchers and ethical boards with respect to advances in technologies and

[1] Data surveillance refers to the process which individualizes each member of the population (or a group), and permits the observation and recording of each individual's activities, then collates these individual observations across the population. From these conglomerated observations, statistical norms are produced relating to any of a multitude of characteristics. These norms are then applied back to the subjected individuals, who are categorized and perhaps acted upon, either with gratification or punishment, according to their relation to the produced norm (Phillips, Privacy Policy and PETs, 2004).

research and the related privacy, data protection, and surveillance concerns that arise with them.
- Policies have to be defined to avoid unethical data mining research.

2.2.6.3 Timeframe for the Grand Challenge Problem

The first four activities can be addressed in a time frame of two to three because they primarily require the application or translation of existing examples or solution from other domains to the educational field. The activities five to seven will require a longer timeframe (3–5 years), as they can only be developed out of the experiences with the activities one to four.

2.2.6.4 Measurable Progress and Success Indicators

A rising number of ethical boards in LA units at educational organisations is a success indicator and presents measureable progress. Other success indicators include the integration of privacy and data protection statements in research projects and between educational providers and students as well the integration of data and privacy competence in job profiles at the educational organisations.

2.2.6.5 Attraction of Funding

Funding for theses challenges could be attracted from EU FP7 projects and the Lifelong Learning Programmes (Erasmus, Leonardo or Comenius).

2.2.6.6 Connected Research Question

- How can different information retrieval technologies be applied to different types of educational data sets to support more effective learning under the constraining conditions of privacy regulations?

2.2.7 GCP12: Open TEL Practices

Effie L.-C. Law, Felix Mödritscher, Martin Wolpers, Denis Gillet and Fridolin Wild

In education, technology is considered an enabler for successful and collaborative activities that supports learners in dealing with the increasing complexity and dynamics observable in all knowledge domains. Although fostered by various

European research programmes, a general shift in funding strategies can be identified. Instead of pushing technologies for organization-driven teaching and learning, more attention is paid to learner-centric approaches that foster competence development beyond immediate domain skills: digital literacy and social competencies prepare and strengthen individuals for acting in digital ecosystems.

Amongst others, EU projects like ARISTOTELE, GRAPPLE (De Bra et al. 2010), IMREAL (Hetzner et al. 2011; Pannese and Dimitrova 2011), MATURE (Kaschig et al. 2010), METAFORA (Wegerif and Yang 2011), ROLE (Kirschenmann et al. 2010), and TERENCE[2] indicate the importance of so-called "transcompetencies", personalized learning experiences, collaboration, and reflection. Other research, for instance in the projects 80DAYS (Law and Kickmeier-Rust 2008), ALICE (Caballé et al. 2011), COSPATIAL (Giusti et al. 2011), GALA,[3] or ITEC,[4] focuses on interactivity of content, educational games, or learner characteristics beyond domain-specific knowledge.

By understanding a learner as an actor in a learning ecology, TEL research has started to capture and analyse the interactions of a learner with her environments, which can be characterised as (ad-hoc) networks of actors, artefacts, tools, activities, and communities. In the beginning, strongly motivated by being a counterpart to managed learning technology, streams like personal learning environments (PLEs) have emerged over the last few years with the aim of empowering learners to design their own environments and to connect to learner networks to collaborate on shared artefacts and goal achievements (Van Harmelen 2008; Wild et al. 2008). EU projects like ROLE, ITEC, and LTfLL[5] have been investigating PLE technologies and approaches.

From a more technical perspective, app and widget technology is being developed and applied for learning in many different settings and for different purposes, as reported by projects like ROLE[6] or ITEC. The overall goal here is to reach a certain level of variability in using technology for learning.

Interoperability has been investigated on different levels and in various EU projects, such as ICOPER[7] or ROLE, as well as in various R&D communities like CSCW, SCORM, or IMS. Basically, these standardisation movements aim at making learning objects, learning designs, and educational scripts accessible for others in order to foster sharing and reusability of educational resources.

One grand challenge in the European Educational Area deals with reaching a certain level of scale in variability, e.g. flexibility of learning technologies, and building capacity for sharing and consuming experiences and practices of technology use in learning and teaching. Variability and the capacity for variability is a

---

[2] http://www.terenceproject.eu

[3] http://www.galanoe.eu/

[4] http://itec.eun.org/

[5] http://www.ltfll-project.org/

[6] http://www.role-project.eu/

[7] http://www.icoper.org/

precondition for a flexibly changing learning environment. Hence, to assist the evolution of teaching with technology, this grand challenge aims at delivering facilities with which a million different (individual) practices describing differing technology arrangements (e.g. a widget space in a PLE) can be shared. It is not an explicit goal to show that a certain practice is used by a million people, but that a million people experience differing, individual needs, and practices in technology support.

2.2.7.1 Problems of the European Education System Addressed and Long-term Benefits for Society

In the European Educational Area, reaching a certain level of scale in variability and building capacity for variability of practices of technology use in learning and teaching still poses a grand challenge.

Though there is a large number of school and university teachers in Europe, sharing practices of technology use in learning and teaching is mostly organised at the institutional, regional, or higher political level.

At the same time, movements such as Personal Learning Environments, standardisation movements for learning resources such as learning objects, learning designs, or educational scripts need to push hard towards interoperability, thereby establishing the means for making large numbers accessible.

Variability and the capacity for variability is a precondition for a flexibly changing educational system. To assist evolution of teaching with technology, facilities for sharing a million different (individual) practices that are supported by differing technology arrangements (such as e.g. arranged in widget-based PLEs) have to be created. This may or may not base on broad socio-technical movements such as social media and web 2.0.

2.2.7.2 Main Activities to Address this Grand Challenge Problem

This includes several necessary achievements:

- Practice capturing and sharing formalisms such as scripts, learning designs, or activity streams.
- Establish facilities to capture context information such as attention meta-data.
- Establish means for interoperability.
- Understand, build, and sustain networks of teachers, including ad-hoc formation and dissolution of such cliques.
- Create large tool repositories such as widget- and app-stores.

Building capacity for variability includes

- Supporting change in pedagogical approaches, shifting the focus from instructional theories and course-based teaching to situated design capabilities and outcome-oriented learning.

- Finding a means of demonstrating evidence to teachers that deploying a specific technology will help them to be more effective in teaching.
- Constantly changing portfolios of tools brings along the danger lacking reliability and stability. Teachers have to be supported in their resilience to cope with this constant change. This may include inexpensive benchmarking methods for assessing effectiveness or efficiency gains that can be achieved with certain practices of technology use.

2.2.7.3 Timeframe for the Grand Challenge Problem

The work could be realised in a time span of 3–5 years. Two main phases can be distinguished of investing into the development of standards plus technology and into the actual gathering of a large amount of practices and contacts.

2.2.7.4 Measurable Progress and Success Indicators

The degree of variability can be studied and measured. There has to be a significantly large number of differences which can be assured by investigating provenance (contributions from all EU countries), position in lifelong learning (school, university, continuing professional development or work place learning), stakeholders (teachers, learners, providers, institutions, policy-makers), heterogeneity in practice (activities supported, different flows for the same aim) and tools (arrangements of widgets, combinations of web apps). Benchmarking millions of people and their associated millions of experiences is a hard target, whereas evidencing a sufficient level of variability could be a surmountable challenge.

2.2.7.5 Attraction of Funding

EU ICT funding should be targeted, as it provides the right mix of research & development combined with strong exploitation and dissemination. Additional follow-up projects in programmes such as the ICT policy support programme (PSP) in its focus on digital content in e-Learning could further the gathering phase. Similarly, EC funding in lifelong learning could provide a source of funding by adding special focus on schools, higher education, vocational education and training, and adult education.

2.2.7.6 Connected Research Question

- In which ways are ad hoc large scale online learning networks of teachers formed and how can the initial formation as well as the sustainability of such networks be supported?

2.2.7.7 Guest Commentaries on Orchestrating Learning

Dr. Volker Zimmermann, born on 3 December 1967, is co-founder of IMC AG. As Member of the Executive Board he is responsible for International Sales (EMEA, SEAP), Mobile Learning Apps and Publishing Solutions, as well as Research and Innovation. Dr. Volker Zimmermann studied business administration at the University of Saarland and at the University of California, San Diego (UCSD). He wrote his dissertation, which was awarded "summa cum laude", in 1998 at the Institute for Business Information Technology (Head: Prof. Dr. Dr. h.c. mult. August-Wilhelm Scheer) of the University of Saarland on the issue "Object-oriented business process management". In 1999, he was awarded the dissertation prize of the Institute for Empirical Economics in Saarbruecken. Dr. Zimmermann has a long history in learning technologies. He has extensive experience in the fields of content production, mobile learning, semantic technologies, adaptive learning both from business practice as well as from academic research. He has written many papers and books on next generation learning solutions.

Ms Diana Dikke, born on 6 November 1986, is working as a research professional for IMC AG. Ms Dikke graduated with diploma in business administration at the University of Saarbruecken (Germany) where she specialised in the fields of information systems in business administration and learning technologies, human resource management, and marketing. Ms Dikke started her work for IMC in 2010 as marketing assistant and holds research professional position since 2011. Ms Dikke conducts research in the fields of competency-based personnel development and learning management, self-regulated learning with web applications, and

virtual learning environments. Ms Dikke is also an experienced specialist in research project and learning software marketing, especially in using web instruments for dissemination activities, as well as web platform administration.

Florian Schultz-Pernice, StD., M. A., formerly grammar school teacher, pedagogical staff member and head of department for speeches at the Bayerisches Staatsministerium für Unterricht und Kultus, now assistant lecturer for media education at the chair of Educational Science and Educational Psychology, LMU Munich.

Jim Slotta is an associate level professor of education in the Ontario Institute for Studies in Education (OISE) at The University of Toronto. He holds the Canada Research Chair in education and technology and directs the ENCORE Lab, a community of researchers and teachers who are dedicated to new ways of learning with technology. He received his PhD from The University of Pittsburgh in 1997, working with Professor Micki Chi, and spent 10 years at The University of California, Berkeley where he developed the WISE (Web-based Inquiry Science Environment) project. His current research employs technology-enhanced learning environments to investigate a knowledge community and inquiry (KCI) model of learning and instruction. He is an advocate of open source materials for the learning sciences, and leads the development of the Scalable Architecture for Interactive Learning (SAIL), which includes an open source "smart classroom in a box" that lowers the bar for investigators to get involved researching and developing learning materials and activities for smart classrooms and knowledge communities.

2.2.8 Guest Commentary by Volker Zimmerman and Diana Dikke

Presently, individual and organisational learning processes are considerably influenced by the rapid changes in the educational and business environment. On the one hand, the need for high-qualified experts increases together with the demands of stakeholders (e.g. business stakeholders, such as employers themselves, their clients and partners, scientific stakeholders, such as universities and institutions, as well as society as a whole). On the other hand, due to fast social and technological development, learners' time-to-competency has to be decreased to ensure prompt employee qualification and application of knowledge. Moreover, there is a need for continuous further education and knowledge transfer, which can be achieved by shifting the focus from curriculum-based to self-regulated learning.

The first attempt to address the outlined challenges was the development of Learning Management Systems assisting instructors in conducting presence and distance classes, and supporting managerial needs, such as learner and content management. With the beginning of Web 2.0 era, multiple tools supporting individual and collaborative learning were created, e.g. learning web applications, multimedia content, and online communities. This led to a new challenge in TEL—a need to provide a framework organising learning resources, services and tools and supporting self-regulated learning by motivating users to mash-up their learning environments and processes themselves.

In order to provide such a framework ensuring individualisation of learning processes and to increase adaptivity and personalisation of learning environments in terms of content and navigation, a concept of *Responsive Open Learning Environments* (*ROLE*[8]) has been created. In this context, responsiveness means adaptivity of learning tools, services and resources according to learners' needs, goals and preferences, whereas openness is directed at open source approach and interoperability issues. Thus, such a learning environment allows users to select, organise, and use learning applications and content to enrich their learning experience in a LMS and to increase effectiveness of the learning processes.

The ROLE approach has been implemented in a concept of *Personal Learning Environment* (*PLE*), which is a learning space where widgets (small web-based applications supporting particular learning and teaching tasks) and widget bundles (sets of widgets) can be added, organised and run. These widgets can be obtained by the learners from web widget repositories, such as ROLE Widget Store[9] offering, in the first line, web applications to support learning and teaching tasks. However, a PLE supports primarily self-regulated learning in informal educational settings, keeping LMS indispensable for more formal curriculum-based learning most common for institutions and organisations.

To address institutional and organisational stakeholders, a pre-defined PLE containing web widgets supporting four learning phases (plan, search, learn, and reflect) has been integrated into the CLIX LMS to create a so-called *Personal Learning Management System* (*PLMS*) combining characteristics and functionalities of a LMS and a PLE. This system supports both curriculum-based and self-regulated learning, thus responding to the needs of organisational stakeholders aiming to make learning processes more user-centred and fitting to individual tasks and goals of particular learners. In a PLMS, the users are able to select widgets and search for learning materials directly in the LMS enriching pre-defined resources according to own learning preferences.

One of the last tendencies on the TEL market is moving from classical eLearning towards mLearning, which means *mobile learning* in terms of used devises and content, as well as flexibility of the learning process aiming to reduce time-to competency in learners' everyday life. The CLIX Mobile app offers a

[8] See ROLE Project, www.role-project.eu.

[9] See ROLE Widget Store, www.role-widgetstore.eu.

possibility to use LMS on smartphones and tablet PCs independent from learner's location or internet availability, as the system can be used in offline modus as well. Further apps designed for iPhone as well as mobile learning games are also already available. Particularity of mobile learning content is not only its special interface design, but more the format destined for short-time learning activities "on the way" making learning with small "learning nuggets" motivating and efficient.

Another approach allowing enrichment of learning content with multimedia objects and supporting "mobility" of the learning process is an *eBook*, a learning medium specially designed for tablet PCs. In an eBook, learning content is represented in a text-form with integrated (original) media, such as videos, diagrams, and soundtracks, allowing avoiding media discontinuity that may result in decrease of learning effect. Moreover, the eBooks aim to increase users' involvement in the learning process and the degree of interaction with the medium making studying with an eBook comparable with a small research. The eBooks can be applied not only in scope of formal learning, e.g. to support employees in learning about new technologies by reading guidelines and manuals, but also on occasion or in informal learning settings in order to close particular knowledge gaps.

Thus, Technology Enhanced Learning experiences rapid development directed on integration of self-regulated learning activities in formal educational processes by means of providing higher adaptivity and personalisation of learning environments, as well as raising flexibility of learning processes as such. The next step in this process will be formation of learning ecosystems creating communities of stakeholders, such as individual and organisational learners, instructors, and learning software developers and vendors, and providing web-based and mobile applications, multimedia content and SCORM-compatible WBTs in one framework, thus allowing users integration of learning activities in their working and social life.

2.2.9 Guest Commentary by Florian Schulz-Pernice

Today's debate about teaching and learning in the field of public discourse and politics as well as in the field of pedagogy and the learning sciences rests on some fundamental assumptions which bridge the gap between the different approaches: Learning is a complex, individual, situated, social, dynamic process. It can be influenced but by no means entirely determined by instructional scenarios. Its outcome depends on the learner—on her cognitions, volitions and emotions. Thus, any attempt to enhance learning—whatever this means in a given context—can best be achieved by providing each learner with a learning environment perfectly adapted and dynamically adapting to his needs in a given learning situation. Last but not least learning as defined also by STELLAR serves a social function—and this is where the inevitable normative aspect of teaching and learning is at stake. Learning arrangements ultimately aim at providing the learner with knowledge, competences and attitudes that are to his or her benefit as well as that of the public welfare.

If we take these assumptions for granted, it naturally follows that technology must ultimately strive to empower teachers and learners to take control of their learning process, not to be controlled by it. This aim is only seemingly trivial. Even if we take into consideration the potential of contemporary ICT to adapt to the individual learner and learning situation, this danger is still imminent, albeit on a higher level of complexity than in the past when ICT was less advanced. From this point of view—and so necessarily from an ethical and also political perspective—, it seems that we have to be aware of and sensitive to the implications of any TEL-approach as to the contribution it makes to empower teachers and learners to design and control their own learning environment.

Seen in this light, some of the ideas outlined in the present chapter seem to be particularly promising. Thus, the idea to provide Semiotic Recommender Systems (GCP10), is an important and very practice-oriented approach of supporting teachers in their attempt to adapt their teaching material to a given situation. Empowering teachers by means of TEL must, of course, be complemented by strategies to empower learners—and here especially the idea of working on Open TEL Practices (GCP12) with its professed aim of helping learners to design their own learning environments seems to be attractive, as well as the development of individual tutors for each learner (GCP8).

However, we also have to see these ideas from a different angle. If we truly confess to a view of the orchestration of learning which aims at empowerment, we must be sensitive to the danger of using technology to contribute to a transformation of learning in undesirable ways. Thus we should be careful not to use TEL to alienate learners from their own learning experience—in this light, GCP6 seems to offer helpful ideas which, however, could also be used to intrude into the learner's integrity if pushed too far. And we should be aware that TEL per se is, often willy-nilly, involved in political issues. If TEL-developments and scenarios offer seemingly simple—and potentially economically lucrative—solutions to problems caused by questionable political decisions, they can easily be misused to justify unwanted policies in the field of education and learning: Developing, e. g., ICT tutoring systems (GCP8) or data supported information systems (GCP9) should not eventually invite political decision-makers to reduce the number of teachers.

2.2.10 Guest Commentary by Jim Slotta

This set of GCP for orchestration has been nicely articulated by some of Europe's most visionary educators. I was a bit surprised by the topics of "emotion-adaptive learning" and "one-tutor per child," but found more familiar ground in the notions of recommender systems, formative assessment, and interoperating educational resources.

One area of common ground was the concern expressed about new forms of educational content that will characterize learning in the coming decades. The nature of this content is changing rapidly, as we are still uncertain about what will be the nature of learning and instruction. Whitelock's call for re-framing assessment from a summative to a more formative and integral aspect of the instruction has been a grand challenge now for more than three decades and remains at the heart of any discussion of learning content. Other challenges, like those relating to tutoring or personal recommender systems, are concerned with the increasingly "personal" nature of content. And as noted by several authors, the shifting nature of our learning designs will require new competencies for students and teachers alike. Hence, the GCP of orchestration seem conspicuously tied to concerns about the nature of learning content.

There seems to be a common emphasis for the need to respond to the depth and complexity of informational resources. Orchestration entails choosing the best possible resources for each learner (or helping them to choose their own), in accordance with the content domain and specific learning goals, activities and interaction patterns. New progress in intelligent tutoring, recommender systems, and real-time processing of learner and domain data (and metadata) will clearly support new instructional approaches. "Smart content" can, in essence, help the teacher in orchestrating complex, learner-centered, formative designs.

One interesting dimension of educational content that was not addressed within the challenges is that of user contributed content. Increasingly, students and citizens are coming to see the Internet not as a place from which they draw content, but as one to which they *add* content. Hence, content is not seen as being static, where pages or other "objects" are retrieved from some vast repository, but rather as dynamic or even *emergent*, as in the growth of a social network, or the accumulation of vote tallies. Such content is reflected in the burst of activity associated with Web 2.0 applications such as YouTube, FlickR, Facebook, and Wikipedia. Open educational resources ("OER"), including user contributed content, may well come to define twenty-first century learning. Imagine a "Wikipedia" brand of textbook, kept up-to-date in all disciplines by a rotating editorial board of educators (with new "problems of the week" added by students or teachers). Open source, negotiated, and comprehensive, such materials could support the development of content communities, where teachers share lesson plans and debate learning scenarios. Imagine such open source text books combined with the PHET simulation library, or a vast array of "Squeak," Lego, or NetLogo student activities.

Another challenge that will be central to the orchestration of any new forms of learning—no matter what forms of content are involved—is concerned with the teacher knowledge that is required for effective orchestration. Often referred to as pedagogical content knowledge, this can only be developed by teachers in the context of real orchestration events. For any given design, what allows one teacher to succeed while others do not? Perhaps good teachers are developing internal models of student knowledge or techniques for evaluating and responding to progress. When moving beyond lecture and lab methods, teachers require time and practice to gain any expertise in the orchestration of new kinds of instruction, including inquiry, collaboration, technology-enhanced or student-centered learning. How can such "orchestrational knowledge" be measured? How can it be sustained, perhaps within a community of peers?

2.3 Grand Challenge Problems Focusing on Contextualising Learning

Learning takes place in a physical, social and historical context, often thought of as 'that which surrounds us', or 'that which is woven together'. As learning takes place, it also creates context meaning that context is continually shifting and being redefined. Digital and mobile technologies provide learners with novel experiences by enabling them to access, contribute to, and operate within, a wider range of contexts than was previously possible. Learners are able to refine contexts to suit their individual needs by choosing and using a range of different tools including social networking and tagging.

2.3.1 GCP13: Learning Reading at Home

Andrew Manches, Sarah Eagle and Rosamund Sutherland

Many technologies to support children's literacy focus on practising specific skills such as phonetics or word recognition, and often do not recognise the important social factors that engage children and bring meaning to reading as an activity. A significant challenge therefore is to examine possibilities for designing digital technologies to foster productive interaction around reading. Designing such technologies requires a thorough understanding of the impact of digital technologies on literacy practices in the home, and the assumptions about literacy learning that lie behind the design of technologies to support reading, and the assumptions that families hold about the use of such technologies. This understanding will then inform the development of a prototype design which can be evaluated in terms of its potential to foster interaction between children and adults (carers, parents, grandparents) around reading in the home.

2.3.1.1 Problems of the European Education System Addressed, and Long Term Benefits for Society

As well as concerns over declining levels of literacy in different European countries, there are increasing questions of what it means to be literate in the twenty-first century. Digital technologies give us the scope to access a wealth of information instantaneously, communicate with multiple recipients from diverse cultures and locations, and increasingly integrate multimodal forms of communication such as video. These new practices have important implications for the design of technologies to foster literacy in the home, where there is potential for discrepancy in emphasis between the literacy practices that a child sees going on around them, and the literacy practices in which parents and others support their engagement. This tension may have a significant impact on the meaning children draw from reading practices in the home.

At the same time, digital technologies are being marketed for use in the home that may be re-shaping interaction between children and the family. For example, unlike more traditional books, digital applications increasingly provide feedback and independent activities for children. More recently, emerging devices such as tablet computers offer new possibilities in the mobility of digital media (e.g. from the bedroom to a train journey) and the capacity to share screens with multiple users. Greater understanding is needed to evaluate what impact these technologies have on the social and emotional aspects of literacy practices.

This grand challenge therefore aims to address the problem of a widening gap between traditional literacy practices in the home and the evolving role of literacy as a result of digital technology.

2.3.1.2 Main Activities to Address this Grand Challenge Problem

The activities will focus predominately on reading practices and can be separated into two main themes. The first will focus on developing understanding of the extent to which young children perceive the role of digital technology in reading practices around them, and how these differ from reading practices in the home. Activities will also explore parents' and grandparents' perceptions of literacy practices and how this relates to support they give at home.

The second theme focuses upon how different digital technologies shape interaction between children and parents/grandparents. This activity will gather information from different sources including comparison of current digital designs and interviews with children and families. This work will lead to the development of guidelines for how the design of programs intended to support reading may affect interaction between children and family members. Finally, these guidelines will inform the design of a prototype digital program on a tablet computer in order to investigate the potential to foster greater interaction around reading in the home.

2.3.1.3 Timeframe for the Grand Challenge Problem

The first theme will involve reviews of the literature as well as interviews with children and parents/grandparents and is expected to take 1 year. The second theme will take 2 years, where the first will develop a greater understanding of the relationship between design and interaction in home settings, followed by the development and initial evaluation of a prototype digital reading application intended to foster family engagement in children's reading.

2.3.1.4 Measurable Progress and Success Indicators

The first theme will result in articles targeted mainly at an academic audience, resulting in peer-reviewed journal and presentation papers. The first year of the second theme will be measured by completion of reports and guidelines for a wider, non-academic audience. Success will be indicated by take up of guidelines in different communities (e.g. designers). The second year of the second theme will be measured by completion of a prototype reading application on a tablet device, and success indicated through evidence of how the design principles are able to foster engagement in reading between children and family members.

2.3.1.5 Attraction of Funding

As well as more general national and European funding sources (e.g. EU, ESRC), funding will be sought from literacy bodies such as the UKLA. In the second theme of this challenge, funding will be attracted from commercial organisations interested in the development of digital applications designed to foster parental engagement in reading.

2.3.1.6 Connected Research Questions

- How can parents'/carers' uses of literacy in their lives become the basis on which they engage in supporting the development of their child's literacy?
- What is the effect of digital reading programs on children's interaction with parents compared to traditional books?
- How can technology be designed to develop literacy practices between parents and young children?

2.3.2 GCP14: Technology for Young Children's Expression of Scientific Ideas

Andrew Manches and Sarah Eagle

Emerging technologies enable new forms of digital representation for children to explore and develop meaning about a range of ideas. In maths and physics, this may be particularly beneficial for young children by building on embodied learning mechanisms and helping draw children's attention to the symbolic aspects of their interactions with materials. For example, focusing on numerical relationships, or physical processes such as Forces. In order to develop these digital representations, it is necessary to develop our understanding of how children's interaction with different materials (both analogue and digital) affect their thinking and how new forms of interaction with technology offer unique learning opportunities.

For younger children, new forms of interaction provide new ways to manipulate, explore, and share digital representations. Tangibles for example allow children to manipulate physical objects augmented with digital technology. These new forms of technology have generated lots of commercial and research interest in their potential to support young children's learning, however, more research is needed to understand the effect of these novel materials on young children's learning. This need would be addressed in this challenge by generating a framework with which to evaluate current designs and identify design opportunities for supporting young children's learning in Mathematics and Physics, then applying this work to develop and evaluate a prototype in this design pace.

2.3.2.1 Problems of the European Education System Addressed, and Long Term Benefits for Society

Comparisons between European nations (e.g. Pisa) highlight the potential to raise children's performance in the areas of numeracy and science. Focussing on children's learning in the Early Years is particularly important given the impact on later achievement.

The potential role of technology for addressing this area has been widely recognised (e.g. Kaput 1992), yet benefits remain unclear, particularly for young children, where there are concerns that everyday technologies such as computers or televisions fail to provide the hands-on, collaborative nature of more physical learning materials. Emerging devices such as tablet computers illustrate how technology is becoming more accessible, and indeed there has been a rapid growth in learning applications designed for younger children in areas such as Maths. Yet, it is not clear how far these designs take advantage of the unique properties of new technologies to facilitate forms of expression in the Early Years. This GCP will provide a framework with which to evaluate current digital representations and inform the design of new materials to support children in Maths and Physics. The challenge will also illustrate the value of this framework in the development of prototypes.

The long-term benefits for society of improving children's ability in Maths and Sciences have been well documented, particularly in economical terms where these areas are key. Importantly, designing new forms of expression for children's thinking may allow more creative expression that has been linked to innovation.

2.3.2.2 Main Activities to Address this Grand Challenge Problem

There are two main activities in this GCP: 1) to develop a framework for evaluating digital representations for Maths and Physics and 2) to generate at least two prototypes in this design space.

The framework will provide a tool with which to evaluate current designs, considering aspects such as: the range of ideas that can be explored; accessibility and engagement; and the capacity to allow children to express their thinking whilst helping draw attention to certain ideas. The framework will be applied to develop guidelines for practitioners and designers in this field.

The second main activity of this GCP will be to develop prototypes; at least one in respective Maths and Physics domains, informed by the framework generated in the first activity. The prototypes will demonstrate how novel forms of technologies (e.g. tangibles/gesture recognition) provide novel ways for young children to express their thinking. E.g. designs for children to build upon their informal understanding of physical forces or numerical relationships.

2.3.2.3 Timeframe for the Grand Challenge Problem

The first main activity will require a year. The first 6 months will involve a review of literature, followed by the development of evaluative guidelines. The second 6 months will be required to refine the framework through evaluations of current designs, and then work with stakeholders (e.g. practitioners) to communicate the guidelines with a wider audience.

The second activity will require up to 18 months. The first 6 months will involve a thorough domain analysis, and identification of design requirements. The second 6 months will be used to develop basic prototypes, and the final 6 months to carry out initial evaluations with designs. The designs will be used as proof of concept illustrations of the potential of technologies in this field; further funding may be sought to forward designs according to evaluation findings.

2.3.2.4 Measurable Progress and Success Indicators

Progress for the first activity will be measured by the completion of an evaluative framework for digital representations for supporting young children's learning in Maths and Physics. The success of this framework will be indicated through successful dissemination in academic fields, and importantly adoption within practitioner and designer communities.

Progress from the second activity will be measured through steps toward prototype development, where success will be reflected in completion of proof of concepts designs. These designs will illustrate the unique opportunities offered by novel forms of technologies, leading to peer-review publication. Greater levels of success will be measured by obtaining further funding for realising prototype designs.

2.3.2.5 Attraction of Funding

Funding applications will be made to national bodies (e.g. ESRC, EPSRC—UK) and to Education agencies for development of practitioner resources (e.g. evaluative guidelines, information resources). Commercial partners will be sought for prototype developments.

2.3.2.6 Connected Research Questions

- What are the limitations of manipulating digital representations through a mouse and how can new forms of interaction address these?
- How can new forms of interaction build upon embodied meanings in children's understanding of physical forces?
- What forms of interaction with digital technologies support early development of number?
- How can new forms of recording (cameras etc.) change children's understanding of knowledge generation?

2.3.3 GCP15: Evaluating Informal TEL

Denise M. Whitelock

As TEL interventions move away from supporting existing learning activities and practices towards disrupting them and/or enabling radically new ones, evaluation approaches need to change accordingly.

By removing the pre-specified design objectives we also remove traditional benchmarks against which we evaluate, such as measures of cognitive learning; while at same time we render evaluation ever so essential in the quest to understand radically new, disruptive TEL practices. We urgently need a re-conceptualisation of evaluation as an integral and integrated aspect of the development process that weaves with evolving designs of learning.

2.3.3.1 Problems of the European Education System Addressed, and Long Term Benefits for Society

With the advent of shorter online courses where any interested parties can participate (see George Siemens' work) and the Open Learn system developed by the UK's OU, a lot of "informal" learning is currently taking place. These technological developments are opening new vistas for learning. The big question then is how to evaluate and allocate credit to this type of informal learning where no prerequisites to join a course are necessary. Informal learning delivered in this way utilizing the latest technological developments requires a new type of evaluation which will assist the learning needs of a changing workforce. Therefore supporting generic learning skills and self reflection will assist an evolving European workforce that can adapt and draw on an e-Learning Society agenda.

2.3.3.2 Main Activities to Address this Grand Challenge Problem

- To synthesise current activity with respect to the evaluation of informal learning and produce a report;
- Construct a set of new evaluation principles;
- Devise a "dashboard" of new evaluation factors to feed back to students to assist their learning;
- Find ways to chart changes in the emotional intelligence of students and how this supports their learning;
- Develop studies that can be funded to investigate the longitudinal nature of disruptive technologies for learning;
- Construct a Roadmap using a Delphi methodology for how technology can assist with this new type of evaluation.

2.3.3.3 Timeframe for the Grand Challenge Problem

The time frame is 2–3 years for the first set of studies but will require 5–7 years for any longitudinal data to be collected.

2.3.3.4 Measurable Progress and Success Indicators

More specifically new evaluation approaches need to:

- evaluate emergent learning in and across formal and informal contexts, as well as the transformation of those contexts effected by the TEL intervention;
- acknowledge that "not all that can be measured counts, and not all that counts can be measured"—look beyond short-term cognitive gains into medium- to longer-term attitudinal, psychomotor, affective, motivational, emotional and behavioural gains;
- look beyond the local impacts of TEL interventions (what this learner learns at this specific moment in time), through their 'glocal' impacts on the surrounding local organisational structures, and further on into their global impacts on the policies and politics of education as well as the formation of social identities;
- see through technology trends and fashions into learners' expectations and how these map onto their actual learning experiences;

- educate learners in the ethical appropriation of TEL;
- make explicit references to their temporal framework;
- be seamlessly built into the TEL intervention and evolve with it.

2.3.3.5 Attraction of Funding

Funding could be sought from a number of charitable foundations such as Gates, Soros as adaptive systems can also support students with learning difficulties. National Research Councils should be lobbied for example the EPSRC in the UK.

2.3.3.6 Connected Research Question

- How can we design adaptive evaluation methodologies and tools providing just-in-time information for evolving designs of online learning environments?

2.3.4 GCP16: Engaging the Brain's Reward System

Paul Howard-Jones

Neuroscience is providing new insights into how games can support effective learning. Recent research suggests games having a special status as an environmental influence on synaptic plasticity, through the rapid schedule of uncertain rewards that they provide. These rewards stimulate phasic dopamine response which, in turn, increases synaptic plasticity and the rate at which we learn. Through a transdisciplinary approach, this project will draw on such insights to generate principles for the design and implementation of educational technology that integrates current understanding of learning games from multiple perspectives. It will implement and demonstrate these principles in a range of technology based applications that raise learning achievement across all curriculum areas, including literacy, numeracy and science. The project will substantially improve motivation and learning of students in European schools by systematically developing and using these game-based environments informed by our emerging understanding of the brain's reward system.

The main goals of the project are:

1. To create new transdisciplinary knowledge about how we can learn through games.
2. To develop and implement a range of content-free games-based learning environments that employ these principles.
3. To evaluate and assess their effectiveness, and demonstrate their potential in terms of measurable improvements in both student engagement and learning.

2.3.4.1 Problems of the European Education System Addressed, and Long Term Benefits for Society

This project tackles the issue of

1. How we can integrate understanding from neuroscience into practical benefits for education, contributing to a science of learning.
2. The increasing "crisis of engagement" faced by teachers across Europe, as they struggle to provide learning experiences as stimulating as the new entertainment technologies.

2.3.4.2 Main Activities to Address this Grand Challenge Problem

The project will involve basic research that focuses on understanding how the brain's reward system responds to different types of feedback—and how that, in turn, influences learning. In addition, it will involve systematic approaches to implementing the outcomes of this basic research in classroom solutions. This will involve a range of different activities including

- The development of neuro-computational algorithms that predict engagement.
- Design-experimentation studies that iteratively develop software-implemented learning principles through a virtuous cycle of brain imaging study and digital design.
- The application of these principles in adaptive game software in ways that maximise engagement and promote learning.
- Bridging studies that study the emerging game designs in the laboratory but also in the real-world environment of the classroom, with teachers actively involved in the process, providing insight and critical evaluation.
- Scaling-up studies.
- Involvement of industry, technologists, educators, neuroscientists to explore the transdisciplinary processes required to build future research capacity.

2.3.4.3 Timeframe for the Grand Challenge Problem

The project can be completed within 4 years.

2.3.4.4 Measurable Progress and Success Indicators

Its success will be demonstrated through measurable improved engagement and achievement among targeted groups of students. In addition, its progress will be demonstrated through the generation of neurocomputational algorithms that have measurable success in accurately predicting behaviour in a variety of game contexts. Alongside these achievements, the project will generate published evidence of the neural correlates of gaming behaviour through brain imaging studies that employ these algorithms.

As well as developing outcomes specific to the technological and educational aims of the project, this work will also involve a reflective component that helps develop, consolidate and communicate good practice in bringing together the fields of neuroscience and technology in applications that can benefit education. These are two rapidly developing streams of influence on education that require novel and thoughtful approaches at their confluence. This project will, therefore, help provide the basis for good transdisciplinary practice that can be transferred to support intellectual and economic enterprise in other areas.

2.3.4.5 Attraction of Funding

Funding for the project may arise from developers interested in commercial products that are educationally more effective than traditional approaches, and that possess a valid scientific theoretical basis for their design.

2.3.4.6 Connected Research Questions

- How can neuroscience help us to understand and foster engagement in learning through the use of games?
- How does this understanding translate into principles to guide the design of educational technology?
- How does this understanding translate into principles for guiding the implementation of such educational technology?

2.3.5 GCP17: Drop-Out Prevention through Attrition Analytics

Hendrik Drachsler

2.3.5.1 Problems of the European Education System Addressed and Long-Term Benefits for Society

A challenging problem for educational institutes and lifelong learning in general are the high drop-out rates, esp. in online and distance education settings. The isolation and confusion of students may cause them to withdraw from their studies. These groups of students are called ‘drop-outs’. The research on TEL recommender systems can contribute to decrease the dropout rate by disseminating its research outcomes for the development of different support systems for teachers and students to offer relevant information at the right time. It is thinkable to develop a drop-out analyzer that informs the tutor of a (Moodle) course which learners are likely to drop-out. This could be done by training a certain recommender technology on the drop-out patterns of previous (Moodle) courses. The trained analyzer could then be applied on follow-up (Moodle) courses and mark students in a list that show similar drop-out patterns. The tutor of the course could then make an intervention and contact those students personally to offer additional support for their studies.

2.3.5.2 Main Activities to Address this Grand Challenge Problem

- Customize existing recommendation algorithms for learning.
- Employ recommender systems in real-life scenarios.
- Develop suitable evaluation criteria for different kind of recommender systems.

2.3.5.3 Timeframe for the Grand Challenge Problem

First implementations recommender systems are already available and can be implemented within a year (Manouselis et al. 2010; Manouselis et al. 2011). A greater challenge is the evaluation of the recommender systems which will take up to 2–3 years. For the further development of such systems, publicly available educational datasets are needed to evaluate and compare different recommendation approaches to gain a solid body of knowledge (5–8 years).

2.3.5.4 Measurable Progress and Success Indicators

Measurable progress and success indicators depend on the applied type of recommender system (curriculum recommender system, drop-out analyzer etc.) (Drachsler et al. 2009). For this Grand Challenge, a significant decrease of the drop-out rate within an educational institution would be a promising measure for evaluating the impact of such a system. A challenging issue will be to isolate the effect of decreasing drop-out rates only to the recommender system as most educational institutes permanently improve their educational services.

2.3.5.5 Attraction of Funding

Aside from European and national funding, such a research project could be funded by single universities (innovation funds) and LMS providers like Blackboard or IMC AG. Next to the commercial providers, recommender projects can be initiated as open source project in the Moodle or SAKAI community, for instance.

2.3.5.6 Connected Research Questions

- How can educational and psychological approaches to the evaluation of processes of collaboration and learning as well as learning outcomes be translated into evaluation measures and metrics for TEL recommender systems that can be applied to every standardized dataset?
- How can educational, psychological and sociological indicators of a high drop out risk, as well as measures potentially able to reduce the risk be effectively used for the design of recommender systems for learning?

2.3.6 GCP18: New Forms of Assessment for Social TEL Environments

Denise M. Whitelock

Our current model for the assessment of learning is primarily summative and individual, firmly bound to hierarchical education structures. This model was developed when knowledge was not abundantly available, when groups of learners were taught and examined at the same time in the same physical location, when teachers and learners were clearly differentiated and when online collaboration and publication were unknown. As new models of learning have been widely adopted, this model of assessment is no longer fit for purpose. A new model is required which takes into account the changes in learning and teaching that have taken place during the last decade.

2.3.6.1 Problems of the European Education System Addressed, and Long Term Benefits for Society

Open, social TEL environments have made new models of learning possible. Learners now draw upon many different people and mediating artefacts, knowledge is dispersed and distributed, individuals may move rapidly between the roles of teacher and learner, and their collaborations extend across time and space. These new models of learning are ill served by a reliance on summative assessment of individuals.

TEL environments also offer new resources in the form of the data they record—learners' demographics, activities, interactions, participation and engagement—little of which is currently harnessed to support assessment. We need to develop ethical frameworks and learning analytics that will enable us to change our assessment practices to support learning in these new educational environments.

2.3.6.2 Main Activities to Address this Grand Challenge Problem

- Learning network analysis—assessing networks and driving the development of groups and networks that provide effective support for learners.
- Learning dialogue—assessing the quality of dialogue, and using this formative assessment to guide the development of learning dialogue.
- Learning behaviour analysis—assessing the activity of individuals and groups, and using this formative assessment to guide the development of skills and behaviours associated with learning.
- Learning content analysis—assessing the resources available to learners, and using this information to recommend appropriate materials, groups and experts.
- Summative analysis of networks, dialogue, behaviour and content that is valued by learners, teachers and society.
- Development of recommendation engines that use these analytics to provide personalised recommendations that support learning and that are valued by learners, teachers and society.
- Investigate and prevent free riding and match fixing.

2.3.6.3 Timeframe for the Grand Challenge Problem

Initial work on learning analytics is currently underway, providing analysis, visualisations and recommendations that support learners and teachers and help to develop meta-cognitive skills, educational dialogue and learning. Within 5 years these initial explorations could be trialled, developed, validated and scaled up for widespread use.

2.3.6.4 Measurable Progress and Success Indicators

Measurable improvements in:

- Engagement with learning—supported by directed feedback.
- Quality of online learning dialogue.
- Engagement with online learning networks.
- Retention—due to appropriate and personalised feedback.
- Class management—due to development of a students-in-trouble alerting system.
- Learners' and teachers' awareness of the value of learning analytics.

2.3.6.5 Attraction of Funding

A potential funder is 'Next Generation Learning Challenges': a collaborative, multi-year US grant programme aimed at dramatically increasing college readiness and completion through applied technology. Grant money is issued in multiple funding waves launched every 6–12 months. Wave 1 included a call to research learning analytics.[10]

Another possible funder is Google, which offers Research award in several relevant areas, including machine learning and data mining, and educational innovation.[11]

While learning analytics can be developed to run on specific VLEs, a large-scale research effort would be needed to bring together different forms of learning analytics and to make them available to learners and teachers working on different platforms.

2.3.6.6 Connected Research Question

- How can we assess learning in open, social TEL environments?

2.3.7 GCP19: Guidance for Technology Use in Early Years

Andrew Manches and Rosamund Sutherland

The proliferation of digital technologies in homes and early school settings emphasizes the need to understand their impact on young children's development. This understanding needs to inform guidelines on evaluating and designing novel technologies.

These guidelines are needed by a range of stakeholders: by parents to inform purchase decisions and value their role in children's interactions with these technologies; by teachers to evaluate designs for learning and know how best to integrate devices into class; by policy makers to inform wider decisions; by designers to inform product development, and by researchers to help illuminate the most pressing questions in this field.

What is missing from current guidelines is a more thorough understanding of how certain digital designs shape children's social and physical interactions. Understanding how novel technologies affect young children's lives requires greater consideration of the role played by traditional technologies such as blocks or books in a range of interactions, in different settings, with a range of actors—from peers and teachers to parents and grandparents. Whilst existing work (e.g. NEAEYC 2011 draft position statement[12]) addresses this area, reference is often made to 'developmentally appropriate' use of technology without clarification of what this entails.

---

[10] http://nextgenlearning.org/

[11] http://research.google.com/university/relations/research_awards.html

[12] National Association for the Education of Young Children http://www.naeyc.org/positionstatements/technology.

2.3.7.1 Problems of the European Education System Addressed, and Long Term Benefits for Society

The current European Education system is limited in providing concrete guidelines for how best to support young children's learning with novel forms of technology. As devices allow more playful, social, physical interaction, this may miss important learning opportunities, as well as fail to take advantage of children's increasing pre-school experiences. Differences in attitudes between institutions have led to significant differences in provision, meaning differences in children's opportunities at a significant stage in their learning.

The main benefit for society of addressing this challenge is therefore to provide those in Education with the information needed to maximize, and thereby provide equal opportunities for Children's learning. Given the importance of young children's early learning experiences on later outcomes, as well as the increasing significance of technology proficiency in employment, supporting young children's use of technology has huge economic implications. Providing usable information for educators will also increase the efficient purchase and use of resources leading to efficiency savings.

2.3.7.2 Main Activities to Address this Grand Challenge Problem

The main activities for this grand challenge can be considered in two main stages:

(1) Summarizing our understanding of how digital technology can shape children's development.
(2) Tailoring this information to specific user groups.

The first stage requires a thorough examination of children's development—including social, cognitive and emotional aspects—and the role of technology. This first stage requires an appreciation of 'traditional' practices such as reading, playground games, role playing and how these are shaped by traditional technologies: such as books, blocks or balls. It is then possible to consider how digital technology presents different opportunities as well as challenges. These opportunities and challenges will be considered in reference to the particular needs of younger children and the evolving nature of digital technologies. Information will be gathered from desktop research and consultation with expert groups as well as an expansive investigation of available technologies and likely future trends.

Having provided a clearer picture of how digital technologies can shape children's development, the second stage of activities involving presenting this information according to the needs of different groups—from those in Education as well as at home, and in industry. Guidelines need to strike a careful balance between ensuring conclusions are well substantiated and that they provide clear and practical advice. In other words, guidelines must be grounded in research whilst offering tangible support to practitioners. In order to support this latter requirement, development of the guidelines will involve regular consultation with the relevant groups (e.g. teachers/designers).

2.3.7.3 Timeframe for the Grand Challenge Problem

The work for this Grand Challenge would take 2 years—with the first spent on the first stage of activities (examination of the opportunities and challenges of digital technologies for young children's development) and the second on developing guidelines (for home, school, policy and industry).

2.3.7.4 Measurable Progress and Success Indicators

The success indicators of the first year will mainly be academic outputs in terms of peer-reviewed documentation summarizing our current understanding of how digital technologies can support young children's development and the possible limitations. This work will also be presented through conferences. In the second year, the first measurable outcomes will be guidelines developed for distinct user groups: parents (carers), educators, industry, and policy makers. The final outcome will be the acceptance and identifiable take up of these guidelines by established communities.

2.3.7.5 Attraction of Funding

European Funding sources would include the European Research Council or organizations such as Marie Curie. A concerted effort would also be made to encourage funding from respective National Research Councils. Exemplar bodies in the UK would be the Economic Research Council. There would also be funding possibilities from different stakeholders such as the Department for Education.

2.3.7.6 Connected Research Questions

- How can technology enhance/inhibit parent/child interaction?
- What is the relationship between early childhood use of technology and child development?
- How are experiences of children with a technology moderated by their local/national culture/community?

2.3.8 GCP20: TEL Plasticity

Effie L.-C. Law, Felix Mödritscher, Martin Wolpers, Denis Gillet and Fridolin Wild

Plasticity of learning environments describes their ability to flexibly adapt (or be adapted) to changing requirements. Learning environments are complex ecosystems. Creating plasticity refers to increased mass individualisation of practices and accompanying technology support.

In recent years, progress towards plasticity has been made in the form of mashup approaches in learning (e.g. in iCamp), sharing facilities (e.g. in iClass), and Web 2.0 interoperability (e.g. Open Social). However, this has been done with sacrifices to user experience and usability.

Nonetheless, increased plasticity will probably aggravate the problems concerning the uptake of innovative technology and practice in learning and teaching. This is already evident in the lack of transfer of skills and practices acquired in the use of technology outside the educational context into learning and teaching. For example, today's pupils are equipped with a higher degree of digital literacy than ever, but they lack practical experience in applying these skills in learning. With the increasing degree of plasticity and flexibility of the emerging learning environments, the issue of being overwhelmed by arrays of choice may become acute.

2.3.8.1 Problems of the European Education System Addressed and Long-Term Benefits for Society

Human computer interaction at large has made a shift over the last years in the form of a so-called third wave that focuses on the creation of user experience rather than just fit-for-the-job technology. At the same time, the opening up of the European educational area to initiatives such as the Bologna process has contributed to a more integrated European education system, in which the learning experience provided by educational institutions is subject to international competition. Fostering plasticity is needed to design for learning by innovating activities, practices, and supporting technology.

2.3.8.2 Main Activities to Address this Grand Challenge Problem

This involves:

Researching and developing means to increase the speed of change and lower the barriers for uptake of innovative practices and technologies. This includes new approaches to support the development of digital literacy of the teachers and knowledge management systems that allow for sharing of evidence that a trajectory is followed that a system has been adapted: providing means to demonstrate plasticity.

Technology can be used as an amplifier to scale up environments. This involves understanding and facilitating the ad hoc formation and dissolution of communities of practices.

Representing change in the mutation of technology and connected practices of learning and teaching forms another focus point. Increased flexibility with respect to pedagogical approaches has to be targeted.

A mixed European community of developers and users has to be created in order to build up the required human capital able to make use of improved means for plasticity.

2.3.8.3 Timeframe for the Grand Challenge Problem

The problem requires action in three areas: improving means for plasticity, supporting teachers (and learners) in the development of new digital literacy required by new practices and tools, and creating a substantial developer-user community to ensure continuous innovation. This could be realised in a 5–10 year horizon.

2.3.8.4 Measurable Progress and Success Indicators

This could be measured via an open market: when e.g. an open market for widgets and educational practices exists (widgets that are embedded in individual practices that are shared), the market decides which ones are best. Digital literacy tests can be developed and integrated into educational benchmarking activities to assess the competence development of teachers and learners. Community size, density of collaboration, traces of use, etc. can be measured, for example, via monitoring relevant existing or newly created social media initiatives.

2.3.8.5 Attraction of Funding

Funding is required for ICT research and development of both educational and technical plasticity methods. EC Lifelong learning funding (and to a limited degree ICT PSP) could support community building and competence development on a European scale.

2.3.8.6 Connected Research Questions

- To what extent do teachers differ in their use of technologies to support learning and how can these differences in their practices serve as a basis for improved adaptivity and adaptability of TEL environments?

- How do communities of practice (CoPs) (e.g., learning communities) evolve once the problems motivating the formation of the CoPs are solved or no longer relevant?
- What are critical success determinants for CoPs? How can these determinants be operationalised in terms of meaningful measures? How can the validity, reliability, and sensitivity of these measures be ensured and improved?
- How can an open market for TEL widgets be created that addresses the different learning contexts and stakeholders?

2.3.9 *GCP21: European TEL DataMart*

Hendrik Drachsler

Define and promote a common generic infrastructure for sharing, analyzing and reusing learning resources and learning activity logs.

2.3.9.1 Problems of the European Education System Addressed and Long-Term Benefits for Society

The increased application of LMS, e-portfolio systems, and PLEs in schools and higher education institutions produces large amounts of educational data. Although these e-learning environments automatically store educational data, exploitation of this data for learning and teaching is still very limited. These educational datasets offer an unused opportunity for the evaluation of learning theories, student support, learning technology, and the development of future learning applications. Furthermore, educational datasets can support research advances on TEL towards a basic theory for TEL (Verbert et al. 2011) by offering the recorded and observed behaviour of the stakeholders (students, teachers, parents, lifelong learners, educational institutes) in different learning settings (formal—informal learning). In that way, the educational datasets extend the methodological and empirical approaches to analyze TEL that is dominated by design-based research approaches, simulations, and field studies (Gray 2009).

2.3.9.2 Main Activities to Address this Grand Challenge Problem

- Data ownership and access rights are challenging because the LMS and PLE systems are collecting educational data and the current assumption is that this data belongs to them. However, the question of who exactly holds the ownership of the data created by the students and what can be done with it is still unresolved.

- Data policies (licences) that regulate how different users can use, share, and reference certain datasets. Until now, there are very limited data policies available in educational institutes. It could be considered to apply the Creative Commons licensing rights as a standard way to grant permissions to datasets.
- Common dataset formats like from the CEN PT Social data group (https://sites.google.com/site/camschema/home) and a standardised documentation of datasets so that others can make proper use of it.
- Methods to anonymise and pre-process data according to privacy and legal protection rights.

2.3.9.3 Timeframe for the Grand Challenge Problem

Anything between 5 and 8 years. For learning resources, there are already standards like LOM and Dublin Core. For learning activities, it's more complicated (apart from very generic formats such as XML—which does not guarantee that data can be reused).

2.3.9.4 Measurable Progress and Success Indicators

- An increasing amount of publicly available datasets and research articles that are based on shared datasets.
- The availability of data or privacy policies at educational providers.
- More data-driven tools at educational providers.
- A common dataset format.

2.3.9.5 Attraction of Funding

Funding can be attracted from governmental funding bodies like FP7, national funding, or funding by companies like Microsoft, Google, or IBM.

2.3.9.6 Connected Research Questions

- How can richer representations of the social context for the use with recommender systems be developed and evaluated with respect to their effects on learning?
- Which new competencies of teachers and learners are required for optimal data-supported learning with recommender systems and new types of data visualisation?

2.3.10 Guest Commentaries on Contextualising Learning

Charles Crook is Professor of Education at the University of Nottingham and Director of the Learning Sciences Research Institute. He is a developmental psychologist with interests in how new technologies re-mediate the experience of learning.

Professor Allison Littlejohn is Director of the Caledonian Academy, a centre for research in Technology Enhanced Professional Learning at Glasgow Caledonian University, UK and Chair in Learning Technology. Allison's research is in the areas of *professional, organisational, sustainable learning* and learner literacies contextualised within public and private sectors with companies including Shell, BP International and Conoco-Philips. Allison was Senior Researcher for Royal Dutch Shell 2008-2010.

Yves Punie is senior scientist at the European Commission Institute for Prospective Technological Studies (IPTS) (http://ipts.jrc.ec.europa.eu) based in Seville. Currently, he is leading the IPTS research and policy activities on "ICT for Learning and Inclusion". Before joining the IPTS in 2001, he was interim Assistant Professor at the Free University of Brussels (VUB) and senior researcher at SMIT (Studies on Media, Information and Telecommunications). He holds a Ph.D. in Social Sciences from the VUB on the use and acceptance of ICT in everyday life also coined as "domestication".

Karen Velasco is a performance management consultant, trainer, facilitator and coach and has worked in learning and development for over 25 years. She is an experienced conference speaker, and her recent projects include research into emotional intelligence, meaning at work, and the use of technology to enhance the learning experience. Karen is the current Chairman of the British Institute for Learning and Development and was recently honoured with an Award for

Outstanding Contribution to the field of Human Resource Development at the 2011 Asia HRD Congress. Karen holds a BA (Hons) in Geography and an MBA (distinction) both from the University of Portsmouth.

2.3.11 Guest Commentary by Charles Crook

2.3.11.1 Varieties of Learning Context

Approaching learning as an experience that is "contextualised" invites consideration of very many research and innovation possibilities. It is therefore not surprising to find a wide (and rich) variety of projects outlined in this section. Although I am not sure that they all convincingly address the theme of context. Certainly, they are all ambitious. So perhaps it is unfortunate that constraints of space mean that the expositions here often need more space to describe clearly the motive, design, and potential of proposed innovation. On reflection, It seems to me that the topic of context invites three strands of thinking—I suggest that two of them are well represented here and a third is under-developed.

The first strand concentrates on the *school*: an institutional context which has been the traditional focal point for deliberate, or formal leaning. But in the background to any consideration of school as context is the prevailing worry that the school is not fit for purpose—even that it is a source of oppressive experiences for the learner. Consequently, several of the proposals here plan to re-fashion schooled learning, perhaps protecting the institution but making it more efficient, more social, more receptive, and more responsive.

To those ends, various digital tools are invoked (e.g., analytics and recommender systems) that will scrutinise the activity of learners in order to tune and direct the character of their experience. There is much potential in such approaches. However, they harbour assumptions about the extent to which the traces of learning activity really will be concentrated within the spaces of a digital infrastructure. They also require a better understanding of how the learner's manifest navigation of this infrastructure co-relates with accepted achievements of learning. These are challenges—but ones worth confronting. A further species of solution to learners' uneasy relationship with schools is to appropriate the structures of gaming. Put crudely: make the experience of learning more 'fun'. It is hard to argue against that ambition. Yet there is a problem of transfer—particularly into working-world tasks that are not inherently motivating or engaging. For instance, writing this commentary is not 'fun'. To be sure, when it is completed I will be glad of the reading it required of me and, perhaps, pleased with the nature of my written response. But if my schooling only prepared me for game-like contexts of learning, I would be poorly prepared for many of the tasks work demanded of me.

A second strand of context involves considering the *domestic* world as a partner to the context of school. Several projects in this collection contemplate how digital tools can become a focal point for interactions that young people may have within their family. There is a long tradition of developmental psychologists studying such interactions in relation to reading. It is refreshing now to see an interest in these interactions as they might be mediated by *digital* tools. Although there is an uncharted problem of how far each generation keeps up with changes in the structure of new literacies and thus how adequate a partner they can be in such interactions

Finally, the relatively neglected dimension of context is that third place we might term "learning in the wild". Learners do not have to locate their activities in *either* schools or homes, technology empowers them to take it into a much wider range of settings—the management of challenges from this contextual diversity is surely one of the Grandest of Challenges in any set.

2.3.12 Guest Commentary by Allison Littlejohn

Identifying how realistic and desirable GCP might be is complex. Every GCP described in this section brings together ideas and concepts from different disciplines to help solve some of the biggest problems associated with human learning. The likely impact of each on human learning is governed by a complex interplay of factors including:

Contextualisation—Groups of people directly involved with each GCP will bring to the project their practices, cultures, and values, grounding emerging ideas and solutions in known ways of learning and working. A high degree of contextualization embeds research and outputs within specific settings, reducing the risk of solutions not being taken up. Conversely, a high degree of contexualisation makes abstraction of concepts to other settings more complex (Boisot 2011b; Knorr-Centina 1999).

Interdiciplinarity—Inclusion of a wide range of disciplinary groups within a GCP enriches the outputs and solutions generated through the project. At the same time, the knowledge generated through the project is likely to be more abstract and less easy to apply directly to solutions across a range of different contexts (Boisot 2011a). Consequently, projects with a greater the number of disciplines tend to be more complex and incur a higher the risk that the outputs will not be adopted widely.

Timescale—The timeframe for the impact of concepts and solution on human learning is proportional to the complexity of the GCP. Complex, interdisciplinary projects will require a longer timeframe for the adoption of solutions, as knowledge is diffused across and interpreted by different stakeholder groups.

Taking these factors into consideration, the GCP can be grouped as follows:

The first set of GCPs is characterised by strong contextualisation, moderate interdisciplinarity and a short timescale. This set includes Learning Reading at Home (GCP13), exploring literacy development grounded within specific social contexts (e.g. reading with grandparents), Technology for Young Children's Expression of Scientific Ideas (GCP14) examining learning through manipulating and sharing digital representations of knowledge and Guidance for Technology Use in Early Years (GCP19). These projects are situated within specific domains with a range of stakeholder groups (children, teachers, parental groups). These groups have well-established practices. Solutions from the GCP Projects can potentially be embedded within these known practices to improve human learning. This process will allow for widespread adoption of solutions within a 'near horizon' timeframe.

The second set of projects is characterised by restrained contextualisation, interdisciplinarity and medium timescale. The projects include: Evaluating Informal TEL (GCP15), Drop-Out Prevention through Attrition Analytics (GCP17) and New Forms of Assessment for Social TEL Environments (GCP18). Analogous to the projects in set one, these projects are situated within specific contexts. Unlike set one, the settings are loosely defined around broad areas—in this case assessment, accreditation and/or attrition. Consequently, project outputs are less likely to be deeply embedded within specific contexts, compared with those from the projects in set one. Conversely, these projects have a (potentially) wider and deeper impact on human learning within a 'mid horizon' timeframe.

The third set is characterized by high risk, interdisciplinary concepts and goals and a long timeframe. This set includes Engaging the Brains Reward System (GCP16), TEL Plasticity (GCP20) and European TEL DataMart (GCP21). The knowledge generated by these projects must be abstracted and codified to allow sharing of knowledge and data across the various disciplinary groups within each GCP. This abstract (largely theoretical) knowledge can be embedded in concrete practice, from which new theoretical knowledge can, in turn, be abstracted. These projects will (arguably) have a deeper transformative effect on learning (compared with sets 1 and 2) over a far-horizon timeframe. However, the diffusion and adoption of ideas and solutions arising from these projects within mainstream practice is complex and risky, requiring a longer timescale than for sets one and two.

In summary, each of these GCPs can impact upon human learning to different degrees. I would like to see more examples of high risk, far-horizon GCPs that establish and integrate research from the physical and social sciences. Bringing these areas closer together could uncover stretch goals—research questions and goals about human learning that we cannot yet predict.

2.3.13 Guest Commentary by Yves Punie

2.3.13.1 Meta-Challenge for Contextualizing Learning: TEL Evidence for Holistic Change[13]

Learning does not take place in a vacuum, and individual learning needs do not arise from intrinsic motivations only. The constructivist view that learning is a

[13] The views expressed in this article are purely those of the authors and may not in any circumstances be regarded as stating an official position of the European Commission.

social and interactive process also acknowledges strongly that learning is shaped by the *context* in which it takes place. As raised in the introduction of Sect 2.3 of this book, digital and mobile technologies are making the range of contexts for learning experiences much wider than they were in the pre-digital era. It is therefore important that a number of Grand Challenge Problems on learning in context.

In this book, 9 GCPs related to technology-enhanced learning (TEL) in context are developed. They are all very interesting and relevant. Reading them, it appears to me, at the risk of over simplifying, that they can be placed under three major headings or themes:

(1) changing education and training systems, including assessment and evaluation (GCP 15, 18 and 20);
(2) understanding new patterns of interaction through the use of TEL, impacting learning (GCP 13, 14, 16 and 19) and
(3) using learning analytics, recommender systems and other learner activity logs for improving learning experiences (GCP 17 and 21).

In addition, two cross-cutting themes seem to emerge: developing digital literacy and, to a lesser extent, addressing differentiated learning needs.

I strongly believe these themes should be labelled as "grand challenges" for current and future learning in Europe and elsewhere. In this commentary, I will only focus on the challenge I think is the most difficult to meet, i.e. how to change the eco-system of learning to embrace new ways of learning and teaching that address the needs and requirements of twenty-first century learning in a networked, digitalized and connected society. In our work at IPTS, we have been advocating the need for a paradigm change in education for some time. During the last few years, educational policymakers, including those at European level, have acknowledged the need to modernize and innovate education and training in Europe. The difficulty is, however, "making it happen".

Some people argue that changing education is like moving a graveyard. I do not believe this to be quite true, as research shows that significant innovative and creative practices have arisen within education and training. The problem is that these initiatives are usually small-scale, local, short-term, not fully recognised and not sustainable. And they often fail to have systemic impact.

Take the case of teachers. There are many highly motivated, creative and innovative teachers who are willing to change but unable to, as they receive no support from the system, or, if you like, from the context they are working in. Holistic change is required (to curricula, assessment, teacher training, teacher rewarding and recognition, school leadership, etc.) and this is what makes change in education and training so difficult and slow. Furthermore, the stakes are high. After all, who wants to experiment and play with the education of their children or with the training of their teachers, without any guarantee of its effectiveness? There is a need for high quality research and for sound evidence which demonstrates not only what works but also what does not work when implementing TEL.

This is, it seems to me, a meta-challenge for TEL research. It must contribute to enabling the systemic change in education and training that is so urgently needed to ensure that current and future learning opportunities are more efficient, relevant, inclusive, innovative and meaningful than they ever were in the past. This means embracing other learning contexts such as the home (GPC 15), informal ways of learning (GCP 13) and also at work, for leisure, in communities (physical and virtual) and especially, while on the move. The latter is a grand challenge that I would have expected to emerge more strongly as regards learning in context: anytime, anywhere learning using mobile and smart devices which enable learners to learn whenever they want and need it, wherever they are.

2.3.14 Guest Commentary by Karen Velasco

2.3.14.1 If We Build It, Will They Come?

The GCPs in Sect 2.3 cover a range of issues affecting the provision of learning across all age ranges, encompassing all aspects of lifelong learning. From making recommendations for the use of technology in early years, through engaging advances in neuroscience to support game-based learning, to considering the plasticity of TEL, these GCPs address many of the issues facing the take-up of TEL across society as a whole.

Recognising the importance of technology in early years' development is vital if we are to create a society where the benefits of lifelong learning are laid-down at an early age and TEL is embraced by all. GCP19 recognises the critical need for clarity in how digital technologies shape children's development, providing pragmatic outcomes for specific user groups. GCP13 and GCP14 follow a similar theme, with the output being a prototype reading application designed for tablet devices and a similar development supporting children's development in maths and physics, respectively.

One of the biggest challenges in any TEL solution is completion rates. GCP17 addresses this, making recommendations for employing recommender systems in real-life scenarios, thereby reducing attrition rates. It is vital that the connected research questions relating to educational and psychological reasons that people drop-out of TEL programmes are also considered as these will provide much-needed input to this GCP.

Effective assessment and evaluation of learning are challenges often raised when referring to informal and/or self-regulated learning, especially when driven by technology. GCP15 and GCP18 recognise these issues and propose commendable actions to address the problems. The activities are highly practical and can be easily integrated into a wide range of learning scenarios in the compulsory, post-compulsory and lifelong learning sectors.

When considering GCPs in TEL it is important also to pay attention to cultural issues. Culture in this context relates to two aspects: the geographical culture that impacts for example, on the propensity to use TEL; and the organisational culture that impacts for example, on attrition rates of TEL programmes. In my experience these two factors have the largest impact on the success of TEL projects. Particularly in corporate learning and development settings, organisational culture has a significant impact on the way in which people take up learning opportunities. For any TEL project to be successful, barriers to access (both physical and virtual) need to be removed; people require support from knowledgeable champions; and staff need to be encouraged and motivated to change the way in which they learn.

Within an organisational setting it is important too, to consider issues around security and the protection of IT infrastructure. Many organisations do not grant their staff unlimited access to the internet—this is not because they believe staff may spend their time '*playing on it*' but more because of restrictions placed on access by what may be perceived as over-zealous IT departments, who are rightly protective of their networked environments and the data contained within them.

Until these cultural issues are taken into account and resolved, TEL, particularly in an organisational context, will not gain the reputation that more traditional forms of learning have.

The GCPs in this section promote some well-rounded research activities to address both the European education system and provide comprehensive long-term benefits to society. The challenge now is to turn these into a reality, with pragmatic benefits for the real world, and making sure they do not just remain an academic activity. In this way, for any future TEL projects, we can be certain that, *if we build it, they will come*.

2.3.15 GCP22: Open Research Methodology Infrastructure for CSCL

Carolyn Penstein Rosé, Gregory Dyke, Nancy Law, Kris Lund, Dan Suthers, Christopher Teplovs and Ulrike Cress

2.3.15.1 Problems of the European Education System Addressed, and Long Term Benefits for Society

In TEL and CSCL, different research groups focus on different aspects of collaborative learning. Some do small scale studies, others have larger samples that allow for longitudinal studies or quasi-experimental designs. The teams focus on different teaching methods (scripting; co-operative learning; knowledge building), gather different kinds of data for their research (text data; video data, log files, performance tests) and apply different methods (interaction analysis; pre-post test designs; multi-level methods).

In order to make use of this variety of research data across the different research groups these relevant data sets should be shared and made accessible. The data sets and related analyses could serve as boundary objects and stimulate fruitful discussion across the different research approaches. Doing so would not only highlight the multivocality in CSCL research, but could also serve as a means for converging evidence about the potentials and effectiveness of TEL and CSCL. Creating such an infrastructure would facilitate the accumulation of evidence about the effectiveness of CSCL in teaching and learning for researchers and the scientific community as well as for stakeholders and practitioners.

Furthermore, sharing of datasets and analyses would ensure that results be easier to validate and replicate, facilitating peer-review and leading to more generalisable results to be shared with stakeholders and practitioners.

2.3.15.2 Main Activities to Address this Grand Challenge Problem

- Development of a technical infrastructure for supporting open data.
- Development of a framework for data sharing. This framework consists of recommendations for technical formats, ethic standards and metadata. It describes the needed preparation of data and the documentation of analyses and results.
- Development of a framework of how to exchange results (both the analyses as replicably performed and their interpretation) and "lessons learned" among researchers, practitioners and stakeholders.
- Build a supportive structure for a dialogical interpretation of the data in order to make the community and stakeholders aware what results converge among the different data sets and different interpretations and to identify open questions.
- Implementation and formative evaluation of this infrastructure.

2.3.15.3 Timeframe for the Grand Challenge Problem

About 3 years are needed in order to develop and implement the infrastructure and achieve a critical mass of relevant data. Existing infrastructures such as PSLC Datashop[14] (Koedinger et al. 2010), MULCE[15] (Reffay and Betbeder 2009), CAViCoLa (Harrer et al. 2007), and Tatiana[16] (Dyke et al. 2009) might potentially be improved upon, adapted or adopted to lessen this timeframe.

---

[14] http://pslcdatashop.org/

[15] http://mulce.org/

[16] http://code.google.com/p/tatiana/

2.3.15.4 Measurable Progress and Success Indicators

- Development of an infrastructure (not just a database, but also communication opportunities, meetings, events etc.).
- Number of shared data sets and different kinds of analyses on each of them.
- Involvement of representative groups.
- Quality of the stimulated discourse.

2.3.15.5 Attraction of Funding

Some core EU-research teams which also integrate research teams from North America and Asia should be funded (by a Network of Excellence or an Integrated Project) which develop the infrastructure, share own data and take the responsibility to make the infrastructure sustainable.

Many funding agencies (e.g. NSF) are increasingly requesting projects to submit a data management plan which describes how data will be persistently warehoused. A platform and infrastructure for sharing could synergistically be funded with such a goal.

One of the challenges—experienced by all existing projects—lies in infrastructure sustainability beyond the funding period.

2.3.15.6 Connected Research Questions

- How can research datasets and analysis techniques be systematically exchanged between research teams?
- Is there a change in the range and type of further research questions through exchange of datasets and analysis techniques?
- How can recent automatic analysis techniques for collaborative learning processes be used to discover the theoretically interesting irregularity in the distribution of data (by helping to distinguish them from measurement errors)?

Chapter 3
General Conclusions

Breakthroughs in Technology Enhanced Learning research are more likely to occur when people come together across the different people-centred and technical- centred disciplines, working on common problems, working as interdisciplinary research teams. However interdisciplinary research is difficult for a number of well-documented reasons. For example in different disciplines, the same or similar terms can refer to very different concepts. Moreover there is sometimes a tendency for interdisciplinary teams to work towards a consensus of ideas, leading to a levelling-out of research results and reports that do not have the 'edge' that is necessary to move the field forward. Disagreements are often dropped from final reports, because of a desire to 'keep all members on board'. We suggest that such levelling-out is not productive, and that it is out of the tensions or conflicts between disciplinary perspectives that innovative approaches and solutions to problems are developed.

STELLAR addressed the challenges of interdisciplinary work by regarding the multiple and complex differences between disciplinary perspectives as essential for innovation. Taking this approach does not imply seeking out differences or tensions, but allowing them to emerge amongst a community in which considerable common ground has been built (Sutherland et al., 2012). Within STELLAR this common ground was provided by three Grand Challenge Themes, Connecting Learners, Orchestrating Learning and Contextualising Learning. STELLAR also developed the idea of an Area of Tension, which first emerged from the STELLAR Delphi study. An Area of Tension is important in that it characterises opposing interdisciplinary views related to future developments in TEL. For example if research within the area *Improving Practices of Formal Education* takes into account the tension *approved practices vs. continuous innovation in the classroom* this may help in understanding a potential barrier to classroom experimentation and innovation, which relates to the view that new technologies should only be adopted in schools when their usefulness for learning has been established.

As a Network of Excellence STELLAR harnessed the interdisciplinary diversity of its partners and stakeholders to produce a set of Grand Challenge Problems (GCPs) in Technology Enhanced Learning research. These GCPs provide concrete, bounded research priority areas that have been identified by key researchers

F. Fischer et al., *Grand Challenges in Technology Enhanced Learning*,
SpringerBriefs in Education, DOI: 10.1007/978-3-319-01667-2_3,

and stakeholders within the TEL domain. They begin to suggest how a future research agenda might be shaped.

This book presents the STELLAR GCPs, organized around the themes Connecting Learners, Orchestrating Learning and Contextualising Learning, together with critical commentaries from stakeholders and researchers. Many of the comments about specific GCPs are relevant to other GCPs in different sections of the book. For example Roy Pea makes the important point, when commenting on GCP2, Technology-supported representation- fitness, that research in this area must engage with the literature on 'learning progressions' within different domains. This comment is also relevant to other GCPs, for example GCP14, Technology for Young Children's Expression of Scientific Ideas and GCP13, Learning Reading at Home.

In her commentary Elisavet Linou raises the issue that the creation of new forms of digital communities may lead to new digital divides. Although none of the GCPs in this book explicitly focuses on this research area, we agree with Grant and Eynon that there is a "need to bring together efforts to tackle digital inequalities and digital approaches to tackling social and educational inequalities within a broader programme of policy and practice that commits to tackling inequalities at every level of society" (Grant and Eynon, 2013).

Florian Schultz-Pernice makes an important point about the risk of using TEL to inappropriately intrude into a learner's integrity and identity. This is an ethical issue and we suggest that in general the GCPs do not pay enough attention to such ethical issues. In a recent report on Technology Enhanced Assessment it has been suggested that "Learning analytics data could have a negative impact on a student's choices and identity when their achievement and characteristics are reflected back to them, predicted and visualized" (Broadfoot et al. 2013a). Related to this Schultz-Pernice draws attention to the fact that the use of TEL in schools is inextricably linked to political issues, such as raising national standards of education.

With respect to technology enhanced assessment Roy Pea draws attention to the importance of the relationship between summative assessment and prospective TEL formative assessment, calling on the emerging field of learning analytics to produce interactive data visualisations for stakeholders. Here again there are ethical issues to consider and we suggest that "Policy makers need to recognize and debate the ethical issues linked to the rapidly increasing amounts of educational data being collected and stored. This should include consultation with parents and young people and centre around issues of young people's rights to access and control their own data" (Broadfoot et al. 2013b).

Whereas the Grand Challenge Problems in this book have been organized within the themes of Connecting Learners, Orchestrating Learning and Contextualising Learning, other organizational categories are possible. For example, these might be: student motivation and engaging the disengaged, improving practices of formal education, assessment and learning, connection between formal and informal learning, teacher training and professional development, early years and technology and learning across the lifespan. Another important category relates to the development of new methodologies for researching Technology Enhanced Learning. For example GCP22 addresses the issue of creating an infrastructure for supporting open data in TEL research. The suggestion is that open data sets and related analyses could serve as boundary objects for constructing dialogue across different research approaches. GCP5 also relates to methodology and addresses the problem that research in TEL should take into account the multiple overlapping layers within educational systems, and the stakeholders involved in such systems, including policy makers, school leaders, teachers and students.

The Grand Challenge Problems generated by STELLAR were written with the idea that they might attract funding for planned research programmes. However we suggest that another way forward would be to open up a competition for a selection of the STELLAR Grand Challenge Problems. Prizes could be awarded for their solution, and this open approach to innovation could lead to fundamental breakthroughs in the field of TEL. The timeframes for such breakthroughs will vary from the short to long term, and as Allison Littlejohn argues in her commentary, it is important to fund high-risk far-horizon GCPs that bring together researchers from the people-centred and the technical-centred research disciplines.

References

Blackwell, A., Wilson, L., Street, A., Boulton, C., & Knell, J. (2009). *Radical innovation: crossing knowledge boundaries with interdisciplinary teams*. Cambridge: University of Cambridge Computer Laboratory

Boisot, M. (2011a). *Collisions and collaboration: The organization of learning in the ATLAS project*. London: Oxford University Press

Boisot, M. (2011b). Knowledge management and complexity. In P. Allen, S. Maguire & B. McKelvey (Eds.), *Sage handbook of complexity and management*. Cranfield: Cranfield University

Broadfoot T, Timmis S, Payton S, Oldfield A, & Sutherland R (2013a), Learning analytics and technology enhanced assessment. Discussion Paper 4: Rethinking Assessment. bristol.ac.uk/education/research/sites/tea

Broadfoot T, Timmis S, Payton S, Oldfield A, & Sutherland R (2013b) Ethical issues in technology enhanced assessment. Discussion Paper 5: Rethinking Assessment. bristol.ac.uk/education/research/sites/tea

Caballé, S., Dunwell, I., Pierri, A., Zurolo, F., Gañán, D., Daradoumis, T., et al. (2011). *Towards complex collaborative learning objects by the virtualization of collaborative sessions*. Paper presented at the 4th World Summit on the Knowledge Society (WSKS 2011)

Conole, G., Scanlon, E., Mundin, P., & Farrow, R. (2010). *Interdisciplinary research: Findings from the technology enhanced learning research programme (2006)*. Economic and Social Research Council; Institute of Education

De Bra, P., Smits, D., van der Sluijs, K., Cristea, A. I., & Hendrix, M. (2010). *GRAPPLE: Personalization and adaptation in learning management systems*. Paper presented at the World Conference on Educational Multimedia, Hypermedia & Telecommunications (ED-MEDIA 2010)

Dillenbourg, P. (2002). Over-scripting CSCL: The risks of blending collaborative learning with instructional design, http://hal.archives-ouvertes.fr/hal-00190230/

Drachsler, H., Hummel, H. G. K., & Koper, R. (2009). Identifying the goal, user model and conditions of recommender systems for formal and informal learning. *Journal of Digital Information,10*(2), 4–24

Dyke, G., Lund, K., & Girardot, J.-J. (2009). *Tatiana: An environment to support the CSCL analysis process*. Paper presented at the CSCL, Rhodes, Greece

Giusti, L., Zancanaro, M., Gal, E., & Weiss, P. L. (2011). *Dimensions of collaboration on a tabletop interface for children with autism spectrum disorder*. Paper presented at the ACM CHI

Grant, L., & Eynon, R. (forthcoming) Digital divide and social justice in technology-enhanced learning. In E. Duval, M. Sharples, & R. Sutherland (Eds.), *A reader in technology-enhanced learning*. Springer

Gray, J. (2009). A transformed scientific method. In *The 4th paradigm: Data intensive scientific discovery*

F. Fischer et al., *Grand Challenges in Technology Enhanced Learning*,
SpringerBriefs in Education, DOI: 10.1007/978-3-319-01667-2,

Harrer, A., Zeini, S., Kahrimanis, G., Avouris, N., Marcos, J. A., Martínez-Mones, A., et al. (2007). *Towards a flexible model for computer-based analysis and visualization of collaborative learning activities*. Paper presented at the CSCL

Hetzner, S., Steiner, C. M., Dimitrova, V., Brna, P., & Conlan, O. (2011). *Adult self-regulated learning through linking experience in simulated and real world: A holistic approach*. Paper presented at the 6th European Conference on Technology enhanced learning: Towards ubiquitous learning

Johnson, L., Smith, R., Willis, H., Levine, A., & Haywood, K. (2011). *The 2011 Horizon report*. Austin: The New Media Consortium

Kaschig, A., Maier, R., Sandow, A., Lazoi, M., Barnes, S.-A., Bimrose, J., et al. (2010). *Knowledge maturing activities and practices fostering organisationallearning: Results of an empirical study*. Paper presented at the ECTEL

Kirschenmann, U., Scheffel, M., Friedrich, M., Niemann, K., & Wolpers, M. (2010). *Demands of modern PLEs and the ROLE approach*. Paper presented at the 5th European Conference on Technology Enhanced Learning (EC-TEL 2010)

Knorr-Centina, K. (1999). *Epistemic cultures: How the sciences make knowledge*. Cambridge: Harvard University Press

Koedinger, K. R., Baker, R. S. J. d., Cunningham, K., Skogsholm, A., Leber, B., & Stamper, J. (2010). A data repository for the EDM community: The PSLC DataShop. In C. Romero, S. Ventura, M. Pechenizkiy & R. S. J. d. Baker (Eds.), *Handbook of educational data mining*. Boca Raton: CRC Press

Law, E. L.-C., & Kickmeier-Rust, M. D. (2008). *80Days: Immersive digital educational games with adaptive storytelling*. Paper presented at the STEG, Maastricht

Manouselis, N., Drachsler, H., Verbert, K., & Santos, C. S. (2010). *Recommender system in technology enhanced learning*. Barcelona: Elsevier procedia computer science

Manouselis, N., Drachsler, H., Vuorikari, R., Hummel, H., & Koper, R. (2011). Recommender systems in technology enhanced learning. In P. B. Kantor, F. Ricci, L. Rokach, & B. Shapira (Eds.), *1st recommender systems handbook*. Berlin: Springer

Pannese, L., & Dimitrova, V. (2011). *Augmented simulated experiential learning: The ImREAL approach*. Paper presented at the eChallenges Conference, Florence

Pea, R. (2007). *A time for collective intelligence and action: Grand challenge problems for cyberlearning*. Keynote address for the National Science Foundation Cyberinfrastructure–TEAM Workshop

Persico, D., & Pozzi, F. (2011). Task, Teams and Time: Three Ts to structure CSCL processes, In F. Pozzi e & D. Persico (Eds.), *Techniques for Fostering Collaboration in Online Learning Communities*. Theoretical and practical perspectives (pp.1–14). Information Science Reference, NY: Hershey

Reeves, T.C., Herrington, J., & Oliver, R. (2004). A development research agenda for online collaborative learning. *Educational Technology Research & Development, 52*(4), 53–65

Reffay, C., & Betbeder, M. L. (2009). *Sharing corpora and tools to improve interaction analysis*. Paper presented at the EC-TEL 4th European Conference on Technology Enhanced Learning, Learning in the Synergy of Multiple Disciplines, Nice

Rowntree, D. (1987). *Assessing students: How shall we know them?*. London: Kogan Page

Selinger, M. (2004). The cultural and pedagogical implications of a global e-learning programme. *Cambridge Journal of Education,34*(2), 213–229

Sutherland, R., Eagle, S., & Joubert, M. (2012). A vision and strategy for technology enhanced learning: Report from the STELLAR Network of Excellence, available at http://www.teleurope.eu/pg/file/read/152343/a-vision-and-strategy-for-technology-enhanced-learning-report-from-the-stellar-network-of-excellence

Van Harmelen, M. (2008). Design trajectories: Four experiments in PLE implementation. *Interactive Learning Environments,16*(1), 35–46

Verbert, K., Drachsler, H., Manouselis, N., Wolpers, M., Vuorikari, R., & Duval, E. (2011). *Dataset-driven research for improving recommender systems for learning*. Paper presented at the 1st International Conference Learning Analytics & Knowledge, Banff

Wegerif, R., & Yang, Y. (2011). *Technology and dialogic space: Lessons from history and from the 'Argunaut' and 'Metafora' projects*. Paper presented at the CSCL

Wild, F., Mödritscher, F., & Sigurdarson, S. E. (2008). *Designing for change: Mash-up personal learning environments*. eLearning Papers, 9

Zhang, H., & Almeroth, K. (2010). Moodog: Tracking student activity in online course management systems. *Journal of Interactive Learning Research,21*(3), 407–429

MIX
Papier aus verantwortungsvollen Quellen
Paper from responsible sources
FSC® C105338

If you have any concerns about our products,
you can contact us on
ProductSafety@springernature.com

In case Publisher is established outside the EU,
the EU authorized representative is:
Springer Nature Customer Service Center GmbH
Europaplatz 3, 69115 Heidelberg, Germany

Printed by Libri Plureos GmbH
in Hamburg, Germany